Am I A
Are You?

Mary Kenny

NEW ISLAND

Am I A Feminist? Are You?
First published in 2017 by
New Island Books
16 Priory Hall Office Park
Stillorgan
County Dublin
Republic of Ireland

www.newisland.ie

Print ISBN: 978-1-84840-624-7
Epub ISBN: 978-1-84840-625-4
Mobi ISBN: 978-1-84840-626-1

Typeset by JVR Creative India
Cover design by Mariel Deegan

New Island Books is a member of Publishing Ireland.

It would be a poor world if we were all the same.

– A guiding principle of my late mother, Ita Kenny

Table of Contents

Actor or actress?

Should women in the performing arts be described as 'female actors' or 'actresses'? In recent times, the tendency has been to use the gender-neutral 'actor'. This has led to some tongue-twisting situations at awards where 'Best Actress' has to be rephrased as 'Best Actor in a Female Role'.

The suffix 'ess' has progressively been dropped from a number of professions, particularly in literature and the arts, such as 'poetess' and 'authoress': these came to be regarded as lesser versions of the mainstream. 'Priestess' was seen as rather more pagan than 'priest'. 'Actress', too, had sometimes been ambiguous: like model, courtesan or prostitute (what we might now call a sex worker).

And yet, women had to earn the entitlement to appear on stage in the English-speaking world: in Shakespeare's time, all actors were male, and it was not until 1629 that the first actresses appeared in the London theatre – and being French – they were thoroughly hissed and booed. 'Woman actors' were disparaged as unwomanly monsters until the 1660s, when 'actresses' were properly permitted to take female roles. That fine Dublin-born actress, Peg Woffington, blazed a trail in the Georgian theatre, followed by the great Shakespearean tragedienne, Mrs Siddons. The profession of actress was hard-won – why not take proud possession of it and own it?

1

A woman is entitled to be called whatever she wishes to be called, and so I sought the opinion of women in the performing arts. Here is Leslie Mackie's response:

'From a personal point of view, I have always preferred to be called an actress. I've been one since I began my career in 1972, and cannot fathom why anyone would change the word, especially those who feel strongly about feminism. I feel it is accepting a subservient role to choose to be called a female actor or even an actor. When I do any newspaper interviews, I always request that I am referred to as an "actress".'

Beth Watson gives a more fluid perspective:

'I always call myself an actor when people ask me what my job is, but I don't mind if the word "actress" is used when people are specifically talking about women in the industry, i.e. the Equal Representation for Actresses campaign.

'I'm in two minds about awards; I think I prefer 'best female actor' and 'best male actor', as it implies that the gender is different, but the job is the same, which is important. I think it has been worth having separate "actor" and "actress" awards historically, because I can imagine an alternative history with only one category in which 'best actor' was almost always given to a man, and women not having a chance at recognition. But I feel like we should soon be moving on from gender-divided awards as we have increasing equality in representation, and a number of non-binary or gender-neutral actors progressing in their careers who cannot be categorised in this way.'

The renowned Helen McCrory likes to be described as an actress. 'I'm not an actor, I'm an actress,' she told the *London Evening Standard*. 'I find it odd when people introduce me as an actor. There are many, many jobs that [sic] it doesn't matter what sex you are – it doesn't matter what sex your doctor is, or your lawyer – but as an actress your sex really matters because [it is] part of your experience of the world is as a woman.'

The MTV Movie Awards introduced gender-neutral categories when Emma Watson won for 'Best Actor' in 2017, but Ms McCrory also fears that should a 'Best Actor' award become gender-neutral, there could be fewer awards, as a consequence, for actresses. This is a key point: it would be no service to feminism if a category-change meant that women then had fewer opportunities.

Choose whatever you want to be called, but it may not be always useful to sacrifice practical career advantages for linguistic ideology. And it shouldn't necessarily be assumed that the feminine suffix 'ess' is automatically inferior.

Agency

This is a very fashionable word in serious feminist discourse. In feminist thought, agency can be defined as the entitlement to exercise one's own free will and to be respected as such.

Free will is also invoked in Christian doctrine. I am all for free will. Except that, looking back on my life, I often ask myself whether something entirely outside my own 'agency' prompted some of the bewildering (and occasionally catastrophic) decisions I made. There were good decisions too, but some perhaps were made for reasons outside of my own 'agency' – duty, care, pity, pride, possibly even altruism. And sometimes, you go with a gut instinct, rather than a rational application of 'agency'.

'Agency' is a worthy principle, and an energetic counterpoint to a certain type of traditional feminine passivity; yet it strikes me as reductive in explaining human behaviour. We are driven by many different needs and motives, and sometimes even genetic predisposition – since some of our traits of character are inherited. As you can usually see in any family history.

We also make certain decisions to please people (or to displease them), out of a feeling that we owe a debt of gratitude, not to cause trouble, to conform with what others are doing (and saying) and, above all, it seems to me, because we need the money. Who would work at half the jobs that must be done if it wasn't for money? Pure theory of 'agency' might assume you are Sheryl Sandberg (annual remuneration: $24 million).

Even given my age and experience, I am wary of persuasive people who I feel will railroad me into doing something I really wouldn't choose to do; I murmur to myself 'They can't make me, they can't make me'. But sometimes they can make me, all the same, and I put myself through ordeals which, if I genuinely had 'agency', I would decline.

Art as a feminist issue

I am at an exquisite exhibition in Paris of the works of Camille Pissarro – whose paintings I find more human than his contemporary, Monet (those endless lilies!); Pissarro had an empathetic eye for market women, peasant girls and the honour due to those who labour, as well as having an inspiring vision of landscape.

It's a well-attended exhibition – as so many are. And in accordance with other gallery visits observed, the attendance is overwhelmingly female. At the Marmotte Museum there are about eight women to every one man. Granted, these exhibitions tend to attract an older cohort (though there are some young people present too), and perhaps the men die off earlier. But it's a pattern I've seen in Dublin, London, Paris, New York, Berlin and Rome, and it's not just confined to art galleries. The tendency is also there at concerts, at the theatre, and at art cinemas, where, if I'm sitting watching a Polish film, two-thirds of those present will be female.

Why are so many women evident at cultural events – so often, indeed, in the majority? The answer: this is where so many women choose to be, and to which so many women are drawn by inclination. That's what people do in a free society: they follow their choices and inclinations. If there are fewer women in politics, in science and engineering or in business boardrooms, it isn't always down to prejudice and discrimination. It is evident that women choose to pursue certain activities because that is what they like to do. There are other areas that they do not choose in significant numbers, and from my own personal experience, they should not be nagged, pestered, harried or coerced into doing so.

Jean Monnet, one of the founding fathers (and that is an apt description) of what was to become the European Union, said in later life that if he had to begin the European project all over again, he would start with culture, not with treaties and institutions. Perhaps the EU would have more culture and less politics and bureaucracy if that had been the case.

When the 'gentlemen's clubs' of St James's in London started opening their doors to women, more cultural activities in literature, art, music, architecture and cinema blossomed. If you want to get women involved in anything, then enhance the arts. Women have significantly enhanced the arts, because it is a sector in which we have usually felt included; imagine how we could enhance the sectors we haven't typically felt included in, such as technology or engineering.

Autonomy

Autonomy – 'self-government'/ 'personal freedom' – and independence have been hallmarks of feminism since the 1860s, when John Stuart Mill published his famous tract on the subjugation of women (the only book from which he made no money); within society, females were struggling for higher education and for rights over their own property and person.

There are epiphanies in life which illuminate an idea. When I was sixteen years old, I was travelling home from Paris by train with my mother, my two aunts and my cousin. There was a woman sharing our train compartment who was travelling alone. She was perhaps in her thirties, and I can still see the pink-purple tweed jacket she was wearing. She was carrying some light piece of furniture – perhaps a collapsible stool, and she had some other luggage with her. But she had such an air of perfect autonomy and independence. A smile played around her lips, though she was perfectly self-contained. She alighted somewhere before Victoria Station and walked off the platform with confident serenity, carrying her possessions. I thought that perhaps she was an artist and the collapsible stool was part of her gear.

Aged sixteen, I thought that she was the kind of person I would like to be, I thought, aged sixteen. Confident about travelling alone, organising my own life.

8

The description of the first woman doctor, Elizabeth Garrett Anderson, in 1866, striding out independently on the streets of London, 'indifferent to being alone and unprotected' is a striking one.

Autonomy is surely a woman's entitlement. And yet when the frailties of old age begin to show, how grateful we become for acts of kindness and support. Then it is that John Donne's 'No man is an island, entire of itself' starts to make sense. Perhaps only a childless orphan living on a desert island (and a particularly resourceful one at that) could achieve absolute autonomy. We are connected to other people and we depend on them; we also have responsibilities towards them. Margaret Thatcher was excoriated for saying 'There is no such thing as society – there are only individuals and their families', and now I see the point of those who disparaged her for saying that.

Autonomy and independence are valued principles of feminism, but our autonomous decisions may be contingent on a whole range of things, from economics to opportunity to helpful support. Sometimes, in extreme old age, autonomy is wholly lost. The psychiatrist Dr Ivor Browne – who was married to the late June Levine, the Irish feminist – says that when this stage of life looms, our wisest course is contentment, acceptance and surrender. Little by little, we may see our autonomy and independence dissolve. Jean-Paul Sartre, the apostle of choice and self-affirmation, became very feeble, foolish and dependent in old age, and his last days were evidence of the contingency of the human condition. Where old age diminishes autonomy, it may nonetheless illuminate the equality of a certain shared helplessness.

Beauty

In contrast to some feminist theory that beauty is a negative confection imposed on women, I see beauty as a gift. It is a great advantage to be born with beauty. However, the 'beauty myth' is a multi-billionaire industry, and the emphasis on appearance can be stressful for young women. I am sometimes glad that at my convent school, 'character' and 'backbone' were – theoretically – emphasised over beauty. But those who had beauty still dazzled.

The French have a beguiling sub-category: *'belle-laide'*, which means 'ugly-beautiful': an appearance that is plain, even ugly, and yet has a compelling attraction.

So beauty can be quirky, and there are many kinds.

Burqas

I have travelled on a London bus, where on occasion, I have been almost the only female on the lower deck not wearing a burqa or a niquab. It is always a little disconcerting to be in a minority of any kind, but it is also a useful learning experience. Everyone should know what it feels like to be in a minority, sometime.

There is a view – reinforced by French, German and Belgian law – that the burqa is oppressive to women. Perhaps it is, but that is for the woman wearing it to judge. The British prime minister, Theresa May, stood up in the House of Commons and said it is a woman's entitlement to wear what she chooses, and it is certainly not for the State to dictate dress codes. Quite so.

Neither is it conducive to social harmony in a diverse society when police arrive at a seaside resort and order Islamic women to remove their burkinis (extra-modest swimwear), as occurred in France in the summer of 2016. The then prime minister, socialist Manuel Valls, sought to illuminate the point by saying that Marianne, the symbol of the French Republic, is bare-breasted 'Because she is feeding the people. She is not veiled because she is free. That is the republic.'

Does being free imply obligatory bare-breastedness? Or does being free mean being entitled to wear what one chooses?

In a free society, any individual is entitled to wear whatever they like; but they are also enjoined to take on the responsibility for the reaction to what they wear. If a woman is asked to reveal her face for reasonable purposes of identity or security, then that is a consequence of covering her face; just as, if a woman is asked not to visit a cathedral in a bikini or other beach-wear (a similar request is made to men in some holiday resorts containing cathedrals), then that is also meeting with the consequences of choice of dress.

But should freedom mean a police force threatening you with a caution if you do not comply? Hardly.

Some Muslim women say they feel 'freer' by wearing a costume which hides their form. I can understand that. To be able to see without being seen may give a person an advantage. However, if the burqa, or other religious dress, is enforced against the wearer's wish, then that is a different matter. The feminist position must surely be that you stand up for your own independent viewpoint. And it is not the business of the State to lay down sumptuary laws.

Byron's Law

Man's love is of man's life a part; it is woman's whole existence.
In her first passion, a woman loves her lover, in all the others all
she loves is love.

That Lord Byron! He's well out of date, isn't he? I thought so.
And then I had the task of perusing the diaries that I wrote
as a young woman. They're shameful. The Cuban Missile
Crisis (which brought our civilisation to the brink of World
War Three) doesn't get a look-in, what with the anguished
deliberations on love and relationships. I shared a London
flat with a highly intelligent and well-educated friend, and
it sometimes seems that love (yearning, repining, striving) is
all we ever talked about.

Jobs and work and even ideas did matter in my younger
self's allusions, but I can see a strong tension between a
desire to be independent and self-affirming, and a need to
be involved in some kind of ecstatic relationship. There is
a duality there, and it must exist for young women today
as it did for young women in my salad days. And young
men? Yes, often, but perhaps differently. Byron's *aperçu* was
patronising, but it should be contemplated just the same.

Chivalry for boys: how to treat a lady

Show proper respect to ladies by giving them precedence or by offering them assistance, etc.

A gentleman sitting next to a lady at table may converse with her even though he has not been introduced to her.

Guests are placed in the position of honour at table and are served first. Ladies are served before gentlemen.

Stand up when a lady enters a room. Remain standing till she is seated. Always be ready to provide a chair for your guest.

When you enter a doorway or a passage in the company of ladies, stand aside to let them enter first. Open the door for them.

When, in the street, you pass or meet a lady whom you know, raise your hat.

It is impolite to speak to ladies with your hands in your pockets.

It is grossly impolite to interrupt or flatly contradict a lady.

When walking with a lady, you take the outer side of the footpath.

If two gentlemen are walking with a lady, the middle position should be hers, because it is the place of honour.

A boy can show gentlemanly training by being attentive to the convenience of ladies in trams, trains, etc. He may assist with luggage, open or close doors or windows, offer a seat, etc., if required.

To force your way into a carriage, ferry-boat, tram, room or hall before ladies who are trying to leave have done so, is stupid and ill-mannered.

In introducing, the gentleman is usually introduced to the lady [so that she has the choice to decline].

If, later on [in adulthood], you smoke, you should ask permission in the company of ladies.

In addressing ladies superior in rank or age, 'Madam' should be used. 'Miss' should not be used except with the surname.

From the handbook Politeness for Boys *distributed by the Vincentian Order to schoolboys in Ireland in the 1950s. Based on the principles of the Renaissance Italian courtier Baldassaro Castiglione, the handbook was first published in Melbourne, Australia in 1939. It hardly seems appropriate for the education of working-class boys, but there's an attractive and aspirational idea of respect.*

Choice

For many women, feminism simply means choice: that you make your own choices about your life, your options, your calling, your destiny, your relationships. Abortion rights are affirmed in the name of 'choice': the banner reads 'My body, my choice'. The notion of freedom of choice is widely supported, and coercion widely rejected. Choice is indissolubly linked with free will. A volunteer is always more dedicated than a conscript: we are (or should be) more committed to what we choose than what is thrust upon us.

But choices may arrive like windows of opportunity in life, and then *pouf!* They're gone. We take a fork in the road, and rarely can we go back to the same circumstances to choose again. I left a newspaper job that had been a successful gig for me, because I was offered more money elsewhere. After a while I felt I had made a mistake. There was no going back. The context and circumstances had changed once again. Another metaphor: we never step into the same river twice.

Not everything is available to everyone, by choice. We choose from a specific range of options, sometimes taking the least worst one. Sometimes we blunder through life, only coming to realise, in old age, what the true route of our lives should have been – had we been mentored better, had we had different luck, happier circumstances.

The coda to choice, seldom advertised, is 'consequences'. We make the choice, we take the consequences. The hardest part of 'choice' can be taking responsibility for what turns out to be a bad decision.

Don't confuse choice with a sense of entitlement – the illusionary notion that we can all have anything and everything we wish for, whenever we wish it. That's 'princess-syndrome feminism'.

Contraception and women's health

In the 1940s (the decade I was born), overseas doctors and trainee medics used to come to Dublin to observe multiparous mothers (mothers with many children and many pregnancies) give birth. Dublin was a centre of medical curiosity due to the high number of poor mothers giving birth for the sixteenth, seventeenth or eighteenth time. From what I have found, medical people love anything complex or challenging, and some of these deliveries were worsened by the fact that these Dublin mothers were poor and undernourished, with some of them suffering from rickets (soft bones as a consequence of calcium and Vitamin D deficiency). It is medically fascinating, apparently, to watch a woman give birth for the sixteenth time when her pelvic area is undersized because of soft bones.

Before the advent of the contraceptive pill (made available in 1961), the medical profession had a rather snooty attitude to contraception. The condom was available (in Britain) to purchase at barber shops, where the coiffeur would offer a gentleman 'something for the weekend, sir?' It could be purchased by mail order and at some pharmacies – though novels, such as Stan Barstow's *A Kind of Loving*, often depict the purchase as an embarrassing ordeal. Barrier methods for women could be accessed through the discreetly placed Family Planning centres. But doctors mostly stood aloof from the procedure; some medics advised the mothers they attended during a difficult birth not to have more children, but the methods to prevent this were left to their own discretion. The medical profession was above mere sex. It was preferred if the 'pox doctor' (those who dealt with venereal disease) was an immigrant – preferably a clever Indian – so that 'you wouldn't meet him at your club'.

Family planning was not included in State welfare plans, nor did it form part of the British National Health Service, launched in 1948. William Beveridge, father of the NHS, was more concerned with increasing fertility rather than controlling it.

All over the medical world, gynaecology (and obstetrics) did not attract a high status: the feminist Vera Brittain, a very important historical feminist figure who wrote *Testament of Youth*, and became the mother of Shirley Williams, described gyn-obs, even in the 1950s, as 'the Cinderella of medicine'. Midwives and nurses were, historically, badly paid, and there was, wrote Brittain, a certain level of indifference towards 'women's problems'.

The health of women, and of mothers, was simply too often overlooked, or accepted as a hazard of being female. Although the NHS did not provide contraceptive services, it was nonetheless observed by good GPs that many more gynaecological problems came to light when women could attend the doctor's surgery without payment. Particularly prevalent was a prolapse of the womb – the outcome of too frequent, or too neglected, pregnancies.

It was the appearance of the contraceptive pill that changed medical attitudes. The pill had to be prescribed by a doctor, since blood pressure and other health conditions needed to be checked before the prescription was issued. Thus, the medical profession was brought into the procedure of contraception and family planning. Medicine's role in the health of women, and of mothers, was now recognised. At last, gynaecology became a respectable medical speciality.

Fertility management was (and is) essential to women's health: without it, poor women were having too many children in dire conditions. A ground-breaking publication that sought to improve the lives of working women (and to which Virginia Woolf wrote an introduction), included this contribution:

> 'I was my mother's seventh child, and seven more were born after me – fourteen in all – which made my mother a perfect slave. Generally speaking, she was either expecting a baby to be born or had one at the breast. Everyone had a lot of children. Some were too poor to let the children out to play because they had not enough clothes to cover them.'

Yet this contributor, a Mrs Layton, idolised her mother. She was a great influence on her life, though overworked and worn down. 'She was kindness itself, the friend of everybody… My mother was everything to me.' When tempted into prostitution, the thought of her mother's values influenced her 'not to do wrong'.

Despite the hardships of these women, and the suffering they endured, they are often honoured many years later. There's many a Dublin taxi-driver who has pointed out a former tenement building as we drive by – now gentrified – telling me that his mother raised fourteen children in the most basic conditions therein. And the sign-off is often by way of a salutation: 'She was a great woman altogether! What love she had for us all!' We should be glad that women's reproductive health is a central element of well-being in our day: but there's a retrospective debt of respect we owe to the valour of so many past examples of Mother Courage.

The Catholic Church's proscription of 'artificial contraception' is spelled out in the encyclical 'Humanae Vitae', issued with great controversy in 1968. The impact that it made most likely advertised contraception more than prohibiting it. We know, from the autobiography of John Rock, the Catholic physician who worked on the pill, that women in Latin America were queuing up to avail of it.

'Humanae Vitae' is an idealistic and poetic document, which invokes the beauty of 'the transmission of life' within the bounds of conjugal love and mutual giving. It is also a thoughtful dissertation on the 'natural law', as so often explained by the neo-Darwinists: that human and animal life has developed and advanced by breeding and begetting.

The Vatican's recommendation of 'natural family planning' has, interestingly, helped to develop more research into cycles of fertility. Recently, a Danish biologist named Dr Elina Burgland has been researching algorithms to track natural cycles and an ovulation-measuring biorhythm which could be operated by an app. It is not yet considered routinely reliable, but it's an interesting field for research, and could permit women to be more in touch with their bodies this way.

But in reality, women's health was often cruelly damaged by the inability to control fertility, and access to contraception is a health issue for mothers, as well as an indispensable part of women's autonomy, respect and dignity. I hope that Catholic teaching will come to officially accept that this is the case.

Division of labour

When Prime Minister Theresa May and her husband Philip appeared on a TV chat show, they talked lightly about 'girl jobs' and 'boy jobs' around the house. This was considered absurd by most commentators.

But the division of labour was for a long time an accepted practice in the domestic arena. There was a tacit agreement: men did the rougher 'outdoor' jobs, while women did the more domesticated 'indoor' jobs. We would regard this as stereotyping today, but within the context of social history, it seemed rational, and, if not equal, at least complied with a notion of sharing duties.

Camille Paglia notes that the frontier states in the US, like Wyoming (the first legislature in the world to grant female suffrage – in 1869), Colorado (1893), Idaho and Utah (1896), where men and women worked side by side, often in agriculture and animal husbandry, there existed a greater sense of egalitarianism between the sexes than the more 'sophisticated' East-Coast American states, where women were more likely to be sequestered as 'ladies'. Mrs Emmeline Pankhurst said that she had never seen more respect and courtesy towards women than in western American states, where they had been so quick to deliver the vote to women.

The Harvard anthropologists Conrad Arensberg and S. T. Kimbell, who observed Irish agricultural families in

1938, also noted that a farm was a cooperative and a family worked it together, each according to their abilities. Men looked after the big animals, and women looked after the more domestic livestock, but they were each aware of each other's contribution to labour.

An element of this division of labour survived into my youth, when my brothers and uncles would be expected to do outdoor chores and mechanical repairs within the house (and garden).

However, when I asked my husband, soon after marriage, to affix a plug to an electrical apparatus, he pleaded specialisation rather than division of labour. 'I don't ask an electrician to speak Serbo-Croat,' quoth he (he was a Balkan specialist). 'Why ask me to do an electrician's job?'

Hilaire Belloc's imperishable quatrain comes to mind:

'Lord Finchley tried to mend the Electric Light
Himself. It struck him dead: And serve him right!
It is the business of the wealthy man
To give employment to the artisan.

In 2017, the insurance company Aviva reported that two thirds of people under thirty-five cannot change a flat tyre on a vehicle, and 20 per cent cannot change a light bulb. Whether these helpless persons were male or female was not disclosed. From the division of labour, we seem to have become an entire cohort of Lord Finchleys!

Divorce

Freedom to divorce has been important to women in individual cases, and as a principle of autonomy and independence. Yet feminism has been usually more concerned with establishing rights for married women than for facilitating divorce.

Divorce in the past could be on unfavourable terms for women, and it often contained a double standard: a woman might be punished for adultery, while a man excused. For a woman to quit the family home when it included children was considered the greatest taboo; the abandoning mother was a scandal. Henrik Ibsen's *A Doll's House,* which premiered in 1879, created a sensation because of this; Leo Tolstoy's Anna Karenina's own moral punishment was her self-destruction under the wheels of a Russian train.

And as divorce was endorsed by systems perceived to be misogynist (and polygamous), some feminists thought that the indissolubility of marriage in Christian European tradition had advantages. (Although America, the land of new beginnings, generally had a less forbidding view of divorce: 1930's Hollywood films like *The Gay Divorcee* were condemned by European Christian leaders as dire American frivolities.)

Winifred Holtby, the influential feminist author (and close friend of Vera Brittain) thought that Christian marriage 'at least gave the wife security – even if it were the security of the chattel'. By contrast, the plight of wives in Islamic societies was made worse by the ease with which they could be divorced. Holtby quotes the Arabian authority Charles Doughty: 'The woman's lot is here unequal concubinage and in this necessitous life a weary servitude. The possession in her of parents [...] has been yielded at some price [...] to a husband by whom she may be dismissed in what day he shall have no more pleasure in her.'

Difficulty in procuring a divorce could also mean a wife could be less easily discarded for a younger model – which happens. One sees a certain echo of this template with the 'Second (or Third) Wives Club' among the billionaires of the United States, where the beautiful young trophy wife is the consort of the ageing magnate, while previous spouses may be consigned to the status of 'ex'.

A conservative but popular Irish female politician, Alice Glenn, said in 1986 to some mirth, that 'women voting for divorce is like turkeys voting for Christmas'. In Ireland, where it took three referenda to introduce legal divorce, feminists themselves were sometimes divided. Mary Cummins, a strong feminist on the staff of the *Irish Times*, wrote a series of articles about marriage in rural Ireland: she was no fan of wedlock, but she concluded that 'divorce for a couple running a small family farm is ruinous'. Mary herself came from a rural background and saw that there would usually be a rural/urban divide on the dissolution of marriage, and so it has proved.

Considering the status of marriage, the focus for feminists was primarily on securing property rights for married women, equal moral standing, access to jobs and freedom of contract. It's a logical (if seemingly paradoxical) step that security of rights within marriage must be established before the dissolution of marriage is sought. The campaign for divorce rights was included in a women's liberation package of independence, choice and the right to make personal decisions, but it seldom achieved the degree of attention given to other subjects, such as equal pay or control over fertility. Interestingly, it is usually men who complain that they feel unequally treated in divorce and custody cases, and the large sums of money sometimes awarded in divorce settlements usually do favour women.

Dress codes

Dress codes? Wear what you like, I say. But be aware that every costume chosen sends a message.

There's an independent parliamentarian in the Dáil, the Irish parliament, who likes to turn up in a sleeveless T-shirt (and jeans) of the kind that a man might wear on a beach, or when he's clearing out the back garden on a summer's day. Mick Wallace also has long blond hair, tumbling down in corkscrew curls over quite a handsome, though not young, face. That's how he chooses to present himself, and so be it. But many people don't like the cut of his costume choice. They feel that it shows disrespect for our national parliamentary chamber and thus for parliamentary democracy itself. It shows disrespect for voters, some say. That's how they interpret such choices.

Same rule, surely, for both men and women. Dress as you like, but be mindful that people will judge you by your personal presentation and will interpret your intentions accordingly. When it was agreed, during a hot summer session, that MPs in the House of Commons could appear without a necktie, it seemed a practical enough measure; but some said that casual attire would diminish the traditions of Parliament, which have a specific rhythm and history. Not everyone feels the same – some would call this modernisation. Dress codes for men, in these circumstances, are often more exacting than they are for women, but the semiotics are the same: what is worn will send a message. When I see a clever young woman, an aspiring politician, appearing on a morning politics programme wearing a skimpy T-shirt which displays her ample cleavage, I don't disapprove, but I do think: 'You're sending the wrong message with your costume choice. Viewers will take you less seriously thus attired.' Though I have often made the same mistake myself.

Equal toilets

There is a regular event in my life where I experience an acute sense of inequality: when I visit the toilet during the interval at a theatre.

It is almost always the same. A long queue snakes outside the women's toilet. While outside the men's lavatories, men dash in and out with alacrity: there is no queue whatsoever.

In the matter of toilet facilities, men and women are seldom equal. But paradoxically, the disadvantages suffered by women are often precisely because the architecture of the toilets is too equal – that is, they are architecturally constructed to be exactly the same. A similar amount of space has been allocated to the women's facilities as to the men's.

Women need different facilities for their needs in this department. Females need many more toilets because each female enters a cubicle – even for a routine wee – while men can quickly relieve themselves standing in stalls.

There's a biological point to be made here. In this area, as in many others, men and women are different, and therefore a rigid attitude to 'equality' – by allocating the same amount of space – is wholly unsatisfactory.

I have queued at ladies' toilets in Dublin, London, Paris and New York. I've paid nearly £60 for a theatre ticket in London's West End – and up to $80 in New York – and still, I'm stuck in a queue at the interval.

There are some locations that are better than others (motorway service stations have clocked the fact that women need more toilets, but airports are not always as intelligently planned). Generally, there are all too many places where the situation is deplorable.

There has been much controversy in the United States about whether transgender persons may use the bathrooms of the sex into which they've transgendered. Frankly, my dear, I don't give a damn. But I would advise any lad who is transgendering into a lass to stick with the male toilets, for the genuine reason of convenience. There have been times when I have been very tempted to nip into the gents' myself, just to avoid the line outside the ladies. (And a couple of times, when I thought no one was looking, I did so.)

We perhaps need another champion of ladies' toilets in the mould of the great George Bernard Shaw, who in the spirit of municipal socialism in late Victorian England, led an excellent campaign to establish public toilets for women. He observed that it was never too difficult for a man to find somewhere to urinate (the French having instituted their useful street *pissoirs*), but that any woman around town might find it difficult to relieve herself. In Queen Victoria's age, this was thought unmentionable, but GBS thought it should be mentioned, and he duly presided over the ceremonial opening of the ladies' toilet in Camden, London, in 1898.

Men and women have different needs. To be equal, the difference has to be addressed.

Equal pay in an unequal world

Who doesn't believe in equal pay for equal work, and work for equal value? It's a fundamental point of justice. Not that it has always been accepted as such. I remember, back in the 1970s, having a debate with an articulate left-wing female friend who argued (in line with traditional trade union thinking) that a male wage was usually a family wage, whereas a female income wasn't expected to carry those responsibilities. Female income was supplementary to a family wage. And anyway, women usually did different kinds of jobs. (See the film *Made in Dagenham* for an entertaining exposition of the trade unions' opposition to equal pay.)

But things changed, rightly so, and the principle of equal pay came to be recognised as a working right. It was one of the Women's Liberation Movement's main campaign issues in the 1970s.

And where equal pay could be implemented within an employment structure – the public service, teaching, universities, and in corporate life, the service industries – the theory, at least, has now been more or less universally acknowledged.

Except, of course, that the world of work changed greatly during the end of the twentieth century and the first decades of the twenty-first century. According to the analysts, 1973 was the peak year (in America anyway) for income equality. Since then, general income inequalities have tended to increase in all industrialised countries. In the United States, the top 10 per cent of earners now average nine times as much income as the bottom 90 per cent, and the top 1 per cent over thirty-eight times more income than the bottom 90 per cent.

The top 1 per cent of US income earners have more than doubled their share of the nation's income since the middle of the twentieth century, and in the 1990s, the income of the ultra-rich 'exploded'.

In Britain, too, inequality rapidly increased from the 1980s, according to the Institute for Fiscal Studies, and most industrial countries saw increases in inequality from the 1980s to the late 2000s. Baroness Wheatcroft, formerly a financial journalist, has stated that in 1998 a management chief would earn about thirty-seven times the average worker. By 2016, this had increased to 138 times.

This, suggests economist Tony Atkinson, is due to a number of factors, including the liberalisation of trade, educational change, labour market change, family employment patterns and government tax and welfare rules. There is also a pattern of 'family polarisation'; there are more families in which both spouses are in work, and more families where no one is in work. Globalisation has also increased the tendency to reward the 'stars' in sports, entertainment, business and academia, while the worker bees stay below par.

When we consider equal pay between the genders, it seems reasonable to place this in the context of the bigger picture of income change. In the 1970s, when those of us involved in the women's movement affirmed the right to equal pay, we did so within structured employment patterns which would have involved both employers and trade unions.

Now that landscape has all but dissolved. The whole pattern of work and employment has been transformed. There are ever fewer jobs with security of tenure and organised pay scales. So many young people (and older people too) work in the 'gig economy' – as self-employed freelances.

In my own trade, journalism, conditions have altered radically, partly because of technology (electronic media replacing print media, and thus affecting advertising revenue). There are undoubtedly much greater inequalities prevailing than there would have been in times gone by – and gender has little to do with it. Media stars may be paid very handsome sums, while young interns may actually be asked to work for nothing; in between, many hard-working journalists earn a modest living.

Some disparities are not a question of gender, but of policy. The BBC pays the 'big talent' loads of money, and pays working contributors as little as they can (or, perhaps, nothing at all. I have been asked to contribute to BBC Radio 4 programmes, but told there is 'no budget' even to reimburse my rail fare).

Yes, there remains average gender gaps in pay. In the United States, for example, it is calculated that women earn about 80 per cent of the male wage. But there are commentators, including feminists such as Christina Hoff Sommers and Hanna Rosin, who suggest that this pay gap is often linked to women's voluntary choices: that women sometimes have other priorities than raw money and that salary-worship is 'male-normative'.

Pay is also sometimes related to risk. A survey of work accidents in egalitarian Iceland between 2003 and 2008 yielded the information that 100 per cent of those who died in work accidents were men. Across Denmark, Finland and Sweden, 1,157 men died at work, as did 85 women. More men work in the open air, in dangerous construction work, at sea and in other fields where they are more likely to be injured or lose their lives. I sometimes watch construction workers in London on buildings or at work on a new railway line (on a separate cultural issue, it fascinates me that where once every voice on a London building site was Irish, now nearly every voice is Polish), and I don't think I have ever seen a woman amongst them doing the most laborious jobs. It would be illegal to discriminate against any female who applied for a job with the digger: we must suppose that not many choose to do so.

Equal pay for equal work is surely a principle to be upheld and honoured. But we live in a world where inequalities of many kinds seem to be increasing. Pay for British nurses in 2017 was exactly the same as it had been in 2009; in contrast, the top price for a London theatre ticket was £97.50 in 2012. In 2016, the same ticket cost £202.25.

The old-style male trade unionists feared that more women in the labour market would be to the disadvantage of working-class men. That has, perhaps, happened, along with a whole kaleidoscope of social change. It's not half as simple a question as it used to be.

Everyday sexism

Laura Bates made a huge impact with her online movement (and later a book), 'Everyday Sexism', being a thoroughly depressing chronicle of the slings and arrows to which (mostly younger) women are subjected to in the twenty-first century. Ms Bates claims that '41 per cent of young women in London [aged between eighteen and thirty-four] had experienced sexual harassment in public spaces' (in the space of one year). Here is a flavour of some of her reports on the subject of street harassment from women who have contributed to her survey:

- 'There isn't a day in south-east London where I don't get shouted at, followed or stared down. It's like a disease.'
- 'The sad fact is that now I just expect to be harassed or followed on my way home from a night out.'
- 'The women in my life tell me to ignore sexual harassment because they went through it too.'
- 'My fourteen-year-old gets cat-called and whistled at so often walking to school she thinks it's just part of life.'
- 'I was flashed twice on my route home, I was groped between my legs in a club, and had a man masturbate whilst telling me he wanted to suck on my tits in the street in broad daylight.'

- 'I was walking home from a grief counselling session. Countless shouted comments about how unattractive I was over the years.'
- 'I am only just a teenager and it's horrifying, especially when it involves grown men honking at me in the dress … I dress appropriately, in fact, even when I'm in my school uniform things like [sexual harassment] happen. It's utterly embarrassing and makes me fearful of things such as rape.'

When I shared some of these reports with women nearer my own vintage, many felt that the situation was a little 'overstated'. When I sought some reaction among Facebook friends, one responded:

'Why is it that these days a wolf whistle is considered harassment; in my day – and I'm not that old – it was a compliment. [It] Might have made me blush but [it] gave me a spring in my step that someone thought I looked good. Why is that sexism or harassment? How many times, after a few glasses of wine, have women the world over discussed who they think is hot at the office/gym etc. Sexist? Just a bit of fun surely. I have a lot of friends many would consider attractive, my son has a stunning girlfriend, but never have I heard any of them complain that stepping out the front door is like entering a sexual minefield as described by Laura Bates. I can't help but feel her tales have more to do with book sales than reality.'

Older women, from what I can gather, don't object to a wolf whistle (as they remember it); writing in *The Spectator*, Miriam Gross, acclaimed *femme de lettres* and noted for her beauty, observed that she couldn't see anything misogynistic about the wolf whistle. 'Personally, I've always been cheered up by it.' Other women I consulted agreed, although they were usually over forty, and sometimes even older. 'When I was young, wolf whistles were normal and no one in their right mind minded,' recalled Virginia Blackburn, the journalist and biographer of Theresa May. 'Once and only once did I experience something very unpleasant: when a man started yelling comments about my body in explicit terms; he did so loudly, it went on a bit and it felt threatening. But that was it.'

Bel Mooney, the *Daily Mail*'s agony aunt, recalled that: 'In my youth wolf whistles were normal, as well as pleasant calls from road workers like, "Cheer up love!" – which always got a smile. That never bothered me at all. I would say (in all honesty) that I did dress quite sexily too. Only once do I recall an overtly sexual comment (from an electricity worker, and involved "plugging in") and that was unpleasant – and ignored.'

Younger women seem to take the issue more seriously. 'There is a big difference between a cat call or the infuriating "cheer up love" (as if anyone has the right to comment on the fact that you are not smiling) and holding a door open (which is nice and something I would do for anyone, male or female),' noted Lucy Grove. 'Women and girls just shouldn't have to be informed publicly that men are noticing or examining them or thinking about "making love to them" (a particularly memorable masturbator on a bus).' Years at school in London 'dealing with flashers, gropers and presser-uppers on the Tube' makes Lucy very glad that Laura Bates has taken up this issue with such success. 'Strange that women never feel the same urge to address men that way: judge, comment, squeeze, poke, show how exciting they find you.

How uncomfortable, self-conscious, angry and vulnerable it can make one feel.'

This experience was echoed by other young women who recall being harassed and followed around by male pests, including ubiquitous 'flashers'. 'I remember on the Tube – we must have been no more than fifteen and still in uniform,' wrote Jade McIntyre, 'one girl in our year grabbed the hand of the man who was groping her, holding it up in the Tube [and] asking very loudly that he removed it from her arse.'

Ellen Grogan felt that these comments accurately reflect the current social perspectives:

'I think of it this way – a man whistling at or talking to a girl about her "tits" shows a man as subject seeing a female as object whom he as male is entitled to comment on because she is a resource for his pleasure! So these are the kinds of assumptions underlying this kind of harassment – obviously it's "wrong" – expresses objectification of women.'

Stella O'Malley, a psychologist working in the Irish midlands, recalled:

'I was wolf whistled and cat called plenty of times and never minded – it was usually cheerful and friendly. I was, however, also flashed at tons of times (looking back, Blanchardstown in the 1980s was a hotbed for flashers! The place was crawling with them). Flashing was really disturbing in my experience – sickening. Whenever I wore a dress that was particularly sexy, I got lots of positive and cheerfully appreciative reactions – which I enjoyed. But then, I also, almost always, would also get some weirdo whispering something disgusting in my ear or pawing me with a leer. When this happened the sun went out of the day and I'd feel like a dirty slut for wearing whatever I was wearing. And I'd also feel furious. The first time this happened I was twelve years old and on O'Connell Bridge in Dublin. It made me feel disturbed and ashamed. I was wearing black leggings and a black jumper with a cat on it (how innocent!).'

I can't say I experienced much sexual harassment as a young woman (except in Italy, perhaps): but then, I was once told by a psychic that my 'aura' sent out the message 'I can look after myself'. But whether it has got worse, or better, over the years – since, say, the 1960s and 1970s when 'the permissive society' first appeared – I do not know. But this is Bel Mooney's analysis:

> 'It seems to me to be blindingly obvious that the ready availability of porn has given men permission to act in the horrible way Laura Bates describes. It's perhaps hard for younger men and women now to realise that when Bob Guccione first (c. 1971) put pubic hair into *Penthouse* magazine (before that, *Penthouse* followed P*layboy* in not showing it) this was a big, shocking thing – as the mag was not considered to be porn, but "girly".
> At that time you bought porn in pornshops, where the front room was mostly for "normal" sex, while the "secret" back room was for harder stuff. To go into a porn shop took a decision. NOW all that is freely available online, and wider society has witnessed a pornification: fashion, films, even extending to language. Who would have known the meaning of "the

money shot" in 1980? Behaviour changes – and so does our acceptance of those changes. (Look how widespread smoking was, for example.) Since viewing porn has become the new "normal" and children accept "sexting" as normal behaviour, why is it so surprising that men and boys on the street and in clubs think women and girls are absolutely up for it, and that "no" is a come-on?'

Social change often involves many factors. Women today may feel more empowered to object when accosted, even verbally. This is good. More sexual candour may have released more inhibitions, but individuals often interpret signs and signals differently.

Everyday sexism: a lighter side

My friend Marjorie Wallace, an award-winning journalist and founder of SANE, has done more good than most of us by changing the national conversation on mental health. She has pointed out that 'there was a lighter side' to the 'sexist' behaviour of yore, now so widely condemned. As a young woman, she told the *Evening Standard* that she loved being a 'dolly bird'. When she was interviewed by the top BBC brass for a TV job, 'Derrick Amoore, the producer, asked if I could show him my legs. I wasn't offended at all.' Why not? She had (and has) great legs.

She successfully rebuffed the advances of a producer of ITV's *Ready, Steady, Go!* who not only said she had to sleep with him to get a job, but showed her the casting couch. It didn't discombobulate her. She went on to many greater things.

Facilitators of emancipation

(1) The bicycle

In her very fine history of the Women's Movement (published in 1928), Ray Strachey nominates the humble bicycle as a major facilitator of women's emancipation. It was not until the early 1890s, she wrote, that the idea that grown-up women could move about freely was generally accepted; the emancipating agent in this reform was the bicycle.

'The women who first began to ride upon this queer machine were thought to be incredibly venturous, and most people also thought them shocking. In the very early days, indeed, when only men's bicycles were made, the enormity of riding at all was intensified by the fact that it had to be done in Bloomers, and the bold pioneers were freely hooted in the street.'

These 'Bloomers' were loose-fitting knee-length garments, like large knickers, invented by Mrs Amelia Bloomer. Ray Strachey goes on to say that:

> They found in it not only what was then thought to be the exquisite pleasure of rapid motion, but also very great practical convenience. They were no longer

prisoners in their own houses; they could spin off, if they chose, as far as six or seven miles away; they could go to the nearest town to do their shopping and they could visit their friends, and be no longer dependent for these joys upon the convenience of the rest of the family, but only upon their own muscles. It was a wonderful change, and one which was rapidly appreciated by all sorts of women who had no conscious sympathy with the Women's Movement at all.'

A little flock of pamphlets appeared encouraging women to 'conquer the world on wheels'. Susan B. Anthony, the American feminist, said that the bicycle 'has done more to emancipate women than anything else in the world. It gives women a feeling of freedom and self-reliance. I stand and rejoice every time I see a woman ride by on a wheel – the picture of free, untrammelled womanhood.'

Amelia Bloomer, who realised that no bicycles could be ridden in the full skirts then fashionable, was an American suffragist who invented the Bloomer as early as 1857 (when women wore bustles and crinolines). Sadly, she abandoned her invention in 1865 as she didn't want to go down in history associated only with Bloomers: she wanted to be renowned for her writings and her 'serious feminist work'. Alas, poor Amelia! Once your name becomes a brand, there is no escaping its notoriety, and while we still have bloomers – at least in the dictionary definition – her other work is lost to us.

The bicycle also emancipated men, especially men of modest means. I heard this from my uncle, born in 1908, who recalled that when bicycles became cheaper, and, priced at twenty-one shillings (£1.5 pence), which was within the purchasing reach of the ordinary man in the 1920s – a chap could ride nearly anywhere at will. A boy could court a girl twenty miles away, and a girl could choose a suitor within a fifty-mile bicycle-riding range, rather than from her own village or townland. The early bikes were bone-shakers – like the rattling 'Penny Farthing'. With the discovery of pneumatic tyres, the bike became a source of sport, of pleasure and of freedom – and is today hailed as a champion of environmentalism too.

(2) Hair dye

Although feminists of the 1930s lamented the appearance of make-up and cosmetics – they seemed to take centre stage in women's magazines when serious-minded feminists would have preferred topics of social welfare, equal pay and the entitlement of married women to hold down jobs – I'd still argue that Miss Clairol enhanced women's personal emancipation.

The French have (as far as anyone can remember) always been adept at using artificial hair colour, and in 1931 an American couple, Laurence and Joan Gelb – charmingly, *gelb* is the German for 'yellow', and thus an allusion to blondeness – were travelling in France and encountered a hair-colouring product called 'Clairol' (*clair* means 'light' in French. They brought it back to America, and after the Second World War, founded the product called 'Miss Clairol', which was to have an instant and extraordinary success with hairdressers, and subsequently, with women choosing to dye their own hair at home.

The advertising slogan to advance 'Miss Clairol' was significant. It said: 'Does she or doesn't she? Only her hairdresser knows for sure.' This was Madison Avenue at its most brilliant, getting right to the heart of social ambiguity and ladylike insecurity. For until 'Miss Clairol' came along, it wasn't entirely respectable for it to be known that a woman dyed (or even 'tinted') her hair. It might be a sign that a woman was 'fast', or even more likely, 'vain'. A damning phrase I often heard dismissed women as 'mutton dressed as lamb' – hair dye was often the reason for this dismissal. To diminish the offence, the offender might call it 'tinting'… Hairdressing salons sometimes had a private entrance for clients who were coming to have their hair artificially coloured so that no one should know that this was their enterprise.

'Miss Clairol' marketed hair dye coyly, but eventually it was undertaken with more assurance, and if it gave women confidence in themselves, and confidence to be themselves, then hair dye was an agency of emancipation. My own hair colour is now probably an undistinguished grey – I've dyed it for so long I wouldn't know – and finally in my senior years, I've found the hair colour that is, at last, 'natural' to me: punk purple.

(3) The washing machine

It's a bright, sunny spring day, perfect for catching up on the laundry. I load the washing machine and switch it on. And every time I do this, I take a moment to wonder and awe at the science, engineering and technology that has delivered to me this fabulous mechanical servant. I simply put the washing on, push the right knob, and it washes the clothes. I take them out and hang them up, and then, perhaps, I do it again with another load of washing. Then I think of all the women throughout history who had to do their laundry by hand, scrubbing away for hours on end, their hands red-raw, washing and rinsing every stained and soiled piece of household, domestic and personal laundry.

I even remember from my childhood in the 1950s when all the washing had to be put through an object called a mangle, to squeeze the water out before hanging out the garments. The oppression of it! The sheer, back-breaking labour involved!

And as if that wasn't enough, there were proud housewives who cluckingly disapproved of neighbours who didn't get the washing hung out on a Monday (traditionally the laundry day). But, bless them, they had to take pride in something, and if they were wearing themselves out doing the washing, perhaps they were entitled to demand some respect from the community for their martyred status. It isn't entirely clear who invented the washing machine: a series of patents were registered from the 1790s with gradual development throughout the following century. In 1876, Margaret Colwin Trumps registered a rotary washer which was part of the evolution towards the modern concept of the automatic washer. Coincidentally (or perhaps not), the development of the washing machine began to make real progress just around the time of Suffragette activity – from about 1904 onwards – and by the 1920s, this wondrous invention was established in the United States and evident in magazine advertisements. It took until the 1950s before most households in the developed countries began to acquire this great innovation. In Dublin, my Aunty Dorothy was considered very progressive and advanced (and well-to-do) when she acquired a twin-tube in the 1950s. This had its own mangle attached and a kind of tongs which lifted out the washed linen. A higher civilisation always depends upon people being released from everyday drudgery. You cannot be a free woman without a washing machine, and each time I see mine (a Miele, inherited from the previous house owner) operating, I count my blessings and mentally praise the engineers who delivered such a miracle. But perhaps you have to have grown up in an era before such benefits were ubiquitous to appreciate just what an agency of liberation they truly are. In the film *Suffragette*, the protagonist, Maud, slaves away in a public laundry for a living – until she gets caught up in the Suffrage movement. Yes, she needed the vote. She also needed a washing machine.

(4) Jeans

George Bernard Shaw campaigned for 'rational dress' to facilitate women's emancipation. It arrived, surely, with the availability of denim. Jeans freed women immeasurably, and put an end to the horror of corsets and girdles, which in my youth still existed in the residual form known as the 'roll-on'.

Faith matters

Virtually all studies on matters of faith indicate that women are more religious than men: the researchers at Pew Research Centre in Washington D.C. have found that 'from Africa to Alaska, the ranks of the faithful are dominated by women.'

Women were early converters to Christianity and became an abiding influence in its development. Even though feminism has criticised and even denounced most religions as 'patriarchal', women tend to outnumber men in the practice of faith. You don't have to consult an opinion poll: you just have to attend almost any religious service and observe.

Some branches of Christianity have practised more equality than others. The Quakers have allowed women to preach since their inception. And many of the early feminists had Quaker connections. Other non-conformists have extended equal opportunities to women: in the nineteenth century, female Baptists evangelised and preached fiery sermons in the cause of temperance. The mother of the late MP Tony Benn was a Congregationalist preacher, and he told me that his politics and moral inspiration came from her. 'You must always do what is right and stand up for what you believe is right,' was the message.

The Church of England (like the Lutheran churches of Scandinavia) is steadily increasing its intake of women into the priesthood – in 2017, it announced an increase of 17 per cent in female divinity training. The consecration of the first woman bishop, Libby Lane, seems to have had the effect of encouraging women into the priesthood.

However, not all female churchgoers want to see a woman at the altar. The Catholic and Orthodox Churches still adhere to tradition by reserving the priesthood for males (and in the case of the Roman Catholic Church, a celibate male). This is a policy that is much criticised, and in practice, any local church is heavily dependent on women for its operational practice.

Since women traditionally sought confession more often than men, it was sometimes claimed that priests were more sympathetic to women, since, in marital problems, they more often heard the women's side of the story. Certainly there was oft-expressed fear among secularist politicians that women had 'the ear of the priests' – one of the reasons why French socialists feared giving women the vote. Secularist historians have also analysed the strictures on sexuality as a conspiracy of control between 'the priests and the mothers'.

In Ireland, women were once proud to be the mothers of priests and the sisters of priests. Women found the female aspect of faith not in the ministry but in Marian devotion and in the lives of the saints. Ireland's growing secularism is changing the configurations of faith practice and challenging Church power – but there are still more women than men at church services.

Family values

'Family values' became, at one point, a kind of code for anti-feminism, and a clarion call to support the traditional nuclear family of father, mother and biological offspring. The gender-theory feminist Judith Butler says we should never refer to 'family', but to 'kinship', and kinship can be based on a much wider network of persons who are not necessarily blood-related.

This is surely the case: I have felt hugely touched by the attachment I have seen between parents and adoptive children. Not all adoptions are successful and not all adoptions have been well-managed (or, in the past, well-chosen), but there are very successful adoptions nonetheless, and I have witnessed the most affecting feelings of love and devotion within adoptive family situations.

Yet if the concept of 'family' is the enemy of feminism, then it is not the first time this has occurred. Almost every institution has at one time or another opposed the family, and tried to destroy it, from early monastic Christianity to twentieth-century Communism, especially in the USSR where children were encouraged to spy and denounce their parents for breaches of Communist ideology. The family survives it all, and most systems that oppose the family usually end up endorsing it, or even 'owning' it.

Families can be supportive or oppressive. Victorian women were often stifled by family convention – poor Florence Nightingale used to watch the clock in the drawing room, ticking slowly by, as she nearly went mad from the strictures of family life. Acclaimed Victorian writer Elizabeth Gaskell lamented that 'gifted women cannot get away from their relations. A woman cannot get away from her family, even in its absence.' Yet women have also benefited from the dynastic power that a family can bestow: queens and empresses ruled because of dynastic family power, and the great abbesses of the middle ages attained command through dynastic networks. Eleanor of Acquitaine was one of the richest and most influential women in Europe as the wife of a French and an English king, as well as being the mother of an English king. Catherine of Aragon surely kept her head from the axe of Henry VIII because she had family ties with the Pope and the Holy Roman Emperor.

Despite Professor Butler's strictures, the word 'family' has survived and is frequently invoked as a largely positive benefit. Political parties and commercial enterprises alike advertise themselves as 'we are family'. (So is the mafia.) Families contain all the light and shadow of the human condition. Women have felt imprisoned by family values, but have used family networks to their own purpose as well.

Fear of feminism

It is claimed that many modern academics are now frightened to express their opinions on feminism (or on gay rights, gender fluidity, or on Islam), according to Professor Dennis Hayes, a founder of Academics for Academic Freedom. They are frightened lest their opinions might be found to be 'politically incorrect' by the feminist establishment and its allies. There is a 'culture of censorious quietude', and academics generally feel it is better to say nothing at all about 'difficult' subjects, not just for fear of being sacked, but for fear of attracting verbal abuse. 'Try arguing that "there are boys and girls", or, as John McEnroe has found out, that there are male and female tennis players. (The veteran tennis ace McEnroe attracted an avalanche of criticism for saying that the best woman player would scarcely make the first 700 among the best men.) Things are simply not discussed, according to Professor Hayes. 'Academics and students ... go silent.' Academics would prefer to button their lips rather than risk trouble among students on their university campuses.

I imagine that there has always been conformity in university life, as elsewhere. There was a time when you couldn't enter certain English universities unless you were an Anglican (and Cambridge University only accepted women on equal terms of merit in 1947). My own experience of life is that most institutions exert a level of 'group-think'. When I was a young journalist in Fleet Street, for example, the newspaper proprietor would not permit the word 'cancer' in his newspapers – Lord Beaverbrook maintained a ludicrously irrational superstition that it was 'unlucky' to mention the word; and everyone conformed. (It was euphemised into 'a long illness'.) Generally speaking, only eccentrics and rebels do not comply with the values that prevail in any given society. 'Political correctness' is nothing new: only the values defining what is 'correct' have shifted.

I think feminism should champion and support freedom of speech and exchange of ideas, and libertarian feminists do. But some would argue that speech is about 'power', and whoever sets the rules for speech has the power.

Feminine mystique

The Feminine Mystique was the book, written by Betty Friedan and published in 1963, that is credited with launching the 'second wave' feminist revolution (the 'first wave' focused on education and the vote; the second wave encompassed everything that we call 'women's liberation'.)

It made a huge impact on me, as I felt it demonstrated how women had been persuaded – swindled, really – into being happy housewives, controlled by the advertising industry, which kept instructing them to bake fake cakes (the cake formula advised adding an egg to the mixture: the egg wasn't strictly necessary, but it made the woman 'feel' that she was baking a cake). It spoke to me, quite probably, because I loathed the notion of being a suburban housewife. I remember giving the book to a woman I knew who was a housewife – evidently with a view to evangelising her into feminism – but it made no impression on her at all. She was actually perfectly fulfilled in her life, which made me impatient with her response – why wasn't she more like me? Many years on, I see that quite simply, people are different. That's what 'diversity' means.

I met Betty Friedan in the 1980s at an Oxford Union debate. She bore a striking resemblance, I thought, to Indira Gandhi, and also to the comedian Les Dawson. I walked with her through an Oxford garden proximate to her hotel, where she suddenly threw up among the plants. 'It's the medication,' she said mid-conversation. She was totally unembarrassed by this event, which would have mortified me. I admired her lack of embarrassment, which was down to confidence. I remember nothing else about what she said: perhaps her book said it all.

The most vivid social illumination of the 'happy housewife' role also occurred in 1963: Doris Day's film *The Thrill Of It All*. It is a half-hilarious, half-ghastly story about the chirpy housewife who accidentally launches a brilliant advertising campaign. She becomes extraordinarily rich and successful for a while – but guess what, her marriage suffers, and a serene resolution is found when she returns to her housewifely duties and the hint of another baby with scrumptious husband James Garner. It is a social document in itself.

F.G.M.: the advocates, the opponents

The practice of female genital mutilation (F.G.M.) has become a feminist (and liberal) cause in our time: the question is why it wasn't anathematised sooner. F.G.M., or cliteradectomy, is a widespread practice among many African and North African peoples, and reading the descriptions of young girls being 'cut' in this manner seems certainly gruesome.

There were objections to F.G.M. in previous decades. In the 1920s, Christian missionaries were trying to halt it, and I have read that some of these missionaries (in particular, American Protestant women) were executed for their endeavours.

Certainly Jomo Kenyatta, who is sometimes called the 'Father of modern Africa', and was a hugely respected figure of African politics and anti-colonialism, excoriated the Christian missionaries for trying to interfere with a tribal custom he regarded as sacred to the Gikuyu people and their rites of passage. In his autobiography, considered to be an epic text of African liberation, he deplores the fact that 'The custom of cliteradectomy of girls ... has been strongly attacked by a number of influential European agencies', including missionaries and medical authorities. He condemns the Church of Scotland Mission to the Gikuyu people, which, in 1929, issued an order that any children attending their mission schools should not adhere to this custom. This, said Kenyatta, created a major controversy between the Gikuyu people and the missionaries, whom he describes as 'fanatics' and meddlers in African culture, a culture that has an elaborate system of rites of passage. (He noted that the matter was even raised in the House of Commons and that Josiah Wedgwood and the Duchess of Atholl spoke against F.G.M.)

President Kenyatta (who died in 1978) describes the elaborate traditions around the procedure of cliteradectomy, and how the young girl is prepared for this operation 'which is considered an act of communion with the ancestral god (Morungu)'

Providing proper steps are taken, he claims, it is safe and healthy, and will not hamper a female from becoming a mother. However, it will usually deter females from masturbation, which, among girls, he considers to be wrong. 'If a girl is seen by her mother even so much as touching that part of her body she is told she is doing wrong. This, among other reasons, is probably the motive for trimming the clitoris,' he wrote. However, masturbation among boys is 'right and proper', says Kenyatta, and helps them to prepare for 'future sexual activities'.

Kenyatta wrote that the Gikuyu people look upon the 'religious fanatics' trying to halt cliteradectomy 'with great suspicion'. He goes on: 'It is the secret aim of those who attack this centuries-old custom to disintegrate (the Gikuyu's) social order and thereby hasten their Europeanisation.'

Kenyatta's words were enough to influence the anti-colonialist thinking in the 1960s when his book, *Facing Mount Kenya*, first had its international publication, with an introduction by the distinguished anthropologist Jacob Malinowski. Cliteradectomy was the culture of the Gikuyu people and those who objected to it were cultural imperialists; Christian missionaries were meddling in Africa and disturbing traditional cultures.

Female, and even feminist, anthropologists, though disturbed by what they saw in this field, nevertheless tended to take the Kenyatta view – if in modified form – that it was a form of colonialism to interfere with an indigenous cultural practice. In a meticulous anthropological study of cliteridectomy, Ellen Gruenbaum describes the operation in distressing detail, which can be done on girls as young as one or two years of age, up to the early teens (fourteen or fifteen), just before they would reach the age of marriage. The operation may be a 'full cliteridectomy' or an 'intermediate' form. The full procedure 'entails the removal of all the external genitalia – prepuce, clitoris, labia minora and all or part of the labia majora – and infibulation or stitching together of the vulva. Once healed, this most extreme form leaves a perfectly smooth vulva of skin and scar tissue with only a single tiny opening ... for urination and menstrual flow.' The 'extremely small' size of the opening makes the first sexual encounter very difficult or even impossible, necessitating rupture or further cutting. In more intermediate procedures, 'the trimmed labia minora are sewn shut but the labia majora are left alone. Reinfibulation is done after childbirth.'

Gruenbaum acknowledges that most western societies are horrified by this operation and many have sought to ban it. But she underlines that it is most often the women who are the strongest advocates of continuing the practice, and although an increasing number of health workers in Africa are now opposed to it, change has nonetheless always borne the stigma of being a form of colonialism, advanced by white missionaries.

And that is one of the reasons why F.G.M. did not become an 'issue' until modern times. Tribe, clan and adherence to family practices – as well as anti-colonialist attitudes – trump feminist concerns over what still seems to us a brutal tradition.

France and feminism

As a young journalist in London's Fleet Street, I misspent many a golden hour of my youth sitting under the portrait of Barbe-Nicole Cliquot (*née* Ponsardin) at the famed London wine bar, El Vino. Every now and then a thirsty journalist would call for another round, or another bottle of 'the Widow', this being the champagne brought to a grateful world by La Veuve Cliquot. Barbe-Nicole was a remarkable person: she was only twenty-eight years old and the mother of a young daughter when left widowed after her husband's sudden death in 1805. Against all advice and in the teeth of family opposition, she insisted on taking over his wine business. She proved to be an astute wine merchant, shipping champagne to Russia and exporting to England in defiance of Napoleon's wars. She became the very template of the successful businesswoman, and the distinctive yellow label still bears the mark of 'the widow' Cliquot. A widow had not been known to mastermind the family business previously, but after La Veuve Cliquot, other champagne houses came to be headed by women as widows: Madame Roederer, Madame Bollinger, Madame Piper Heisack.

During the eighteenth century, aristocratic women in France had enjoyed remarkable freedom and political influence: they ran the literary and intellectual salons, and often ran the men too, both as independent thinkers and as wives and mistresses. Voltaire's mistress, Madame de Chatelet, was an outstanding scientist who sadly died prematurely in childbirth. French women writers had made their mark with Madame de la Fayette and Germaine de Stael. The painter Madame Vigée le Brun (whose portraits of Queen Marie Antoinette were such a witness to history) said: 'The women reigned then – the Revolution dethroned them.'

There were many French women writing feminist books and tracts: Madamede Puisieux, Madame Gacon-Dufour, Madame de Coicy, Madame d'Epinay, Madame de Genlis, Madame Roland, and most notably Olympe de Gouges, who wrote *Les Droits de la Femme* in 1791.

Napoleon, perhaps on account of being a traditional Corsican, disapproved of women's liberation in any form and thought that women had run wild during the revolutionary period. His 'Code Napoleon' reinstated the double standard whereby a wife convicted of adultery could be sentenced to two years' imprisonment and divorced, but an adulterous husband faced no charge (and scant social disapproval).

But despite his more conservative measures, there was always in France a notion of liberty, especially among intellectuals and bohemians, and the novelist Georges Sand, cross-dressing in the 1830s, emblemised it. Madame Sand only took up wearing trousers because they were so much more convenient than crinolines, and gave the wearer freedom to wander around Paris at night with her mates – she wasn't, actually, a particularly masculine kind of woman otherwise (she was a particularly maternal kind of woman, and her love for Chopin was strikingly motherly).

The University of Paris, the Sorbonne, also admitted women to study medicine well before British (or American) medical schools: Elizabeth Blackwell and Elizabeth Garret Anderson were able to qualify as doctors in Paris from the 1860s (to its credit, Dublin opened its College of Surgeons to women in

1878, the first medical school then in the United Kingdom to do so). The Empress Eugenie, wife of Napoleon III (and a close friend of Queen Victoria), had the casting vote to approve of women as doctors, and duly did so. Women became barristers in France – in 1900 – before any other European country.

Arguably, the first woman journalist was a Frenchwoman, Christian de Pisan (died 1430), court writer to Charles VII. On rather a different note, most of the saints venerated at my convent school were French – Joan of Arc, Bernadette of Lourdes, Catherine Labouré of the Miraculous Medal and Thérèse of Lisieux. Secular or not, France produced young women who affirmed their vision and their vocation, and often did so against official disapproval. A new 'globalised' history of France, published in 2017, nominates the apparition at Lourdes (to Bernadette Soubirous) as one of the most significant events of the nineteenth century, because of its huge narrative impact.

And yet, for all this, France was exceptionally tardy in granting women the vote. Full male suffrage was passed in 1848, but it took nearly another 100 years before French women voted, in 1944–45, a measure passed by decree by General de Gaulle, a republican, but in many social areas, a conservative.

Why did the female vote in France take so long? Strangely enough, because male enfranchisement had occurred in 1848, French women suffragists found few allies among men, and male radicals were highly suspicious of female activists. In 1900, there were seventeen women's rights organisations, according to Felicity Gordon's fine biography of the French feminist Madeleine Pelletier. But they were often divided between socialist, middle-class, militant and moderate. Madeleine Pelletier was amazed at what British Suffragettes were achieving in the 1900s – the unity and discipline achieved, and the way in which women of different classes were marching shoulder to shoulder (mustering a demonstration of 500,000 in one instance). Among Frenchwomen, middle-class women and working-class women, did not find common ground. French socialists were not at all enthusiastic about women's suffrage – the socialist revolution came first, and anyway, they believed that women's wages would undercut those of men. This was in line with prominent women socialists elsewhere – Rosa Luxembourg and Beatrice Webb were also against women's suffrage.

As in Britain, the First World War provided employment opportunities for women – as metalworkers, chemists, drivers of trams. It seemed that women in France would obtain the vote after the First World War – as British women did – but because France lost such a catastrophic number of men in that conflict, a great imbalance in the sexes emerged; the Left feared that the widows and mothers plunged into grief would be inclined to vote conservatively. When Pope Benedict XV expressed his approval of giving women the vote, left-wing suspicions were aroused. Women might be too inclined to vote as the priests urged them. The vote was rebuffed by the Chambre de Députés in 1922.

There were other issues too. Until 1965, women in France were not permitted to have chequebooks of their own. Until 1968, the 1920 law against contraception was not repealed. It hadn't been too literally observed, but it had remained on the statute books for more than forty years: the fear of depopulation went deep.

Simone de Beauvoir certainly galvanised feminism for French women – and for women around the world – with *The Second Sex*, first published in 1949. And then a subsequent Simone, Simone Veil, became the foremost French female politician of her time, and champion of women's rights, interred with full State honours at the Pantheon in 2017.

Gender-neutral language

The British Medical Association has ruled that pregnant women should not be called 'expectant mothers', because describing a 'pregnant person' as female might offend transgender people.

Motherhood, which has been exclusive to females since the dawn of time and the appearance of the human (and mammal) species, must now be shared by any other gender which claims it.

The idea that mothers are always women is being challenged, and will, perhaps, soon be bypassed. A woman who is transgendering to become a man, Hayden Cross, halted her procedure for an interval long enough for her/him to have a baby. The construction of an artificial womb – which may be transplanted into individuals born as male – may very soon occur.

Malta, like some other legislatures, has expunged the words 'mother' and 'father' from their statute books, to be replaced by the gender-neutral 'parents'. Some people will think this progressive; some women may feel that something which has been so exclusive to women throughout the ages (and if we judge by painting, honoured and admired) has been removed from our possession.

(2)

When a senior police officer calls her 'darling' – in that excellent BBC drama *Line of Duty* – DS Kate Fleming suggests that he should use 'gender-neutral' language to her.

Strictly speaking, 'darling' is entirely 'gender-neutral'. You can say it to a man, a woman or a transgendering person moving either which way.

But I suppose, in practice, it is more often used towards women, and DS Fleming (the impressive Vicki McClure) was correct in assuming, far too patronisingly. Older women get these endearments quite a lot, from perfect strangers: 'dearie', 'my dear', 'my darling', and most of the time, we don't like it. I sometimes reply in like mode, with a 'darling' or 'sweetie' to the interlocateur, although occasionally I button my lip if I think I'll seem too much like a sour old dame to a stranger who may only be trying to kind.

Allow me to cite Princess Anne, only daughter of Elizabeth II, who often comes out with non-nonsense responses.

She was once faced with a barrage of paparazzi taking a picture of her (as she dismounted from a horse).

'Look this way, love,' one of the snappers called out.

'I am not your love,' HRH replied icily. 'I am your Royal Highness.'

Alas, we can hardly follow her example in this, not being royal highnesses, but she struck a small blow against being patronised just the same.

Germaine Greer was also empowered to deliver a similar robust correction. On a BBC discussion programme, someone daring to contradict her, began, 'Look, Germaine...'

'It's Dr Greer to you,' she told him authoritatively.

Doctor: yes, that's gender-neutral language.

Gender pay-gaps

Women's rights organisations have been campaigning for some time to 'close the gender pay-gap'. Even Bill Clinton was at it, in his State of the Union address back in 1999, saying he was proud of the progress women's pay had made, 'but 75 cents on the dollar is still only three-quarters of the way there, and Americans can't be satisfied until we're all the way there.' The ideal is that there should be no 'gender pay-gap' between the sexes, and if there is, the presumption is that this is because of discrimination and prejudice.

But Dr Joanna Williams of Canterbury University, in her incisive book, *Women versus Feminism*, suggests that many myths abound in this area. While in the UK women are said to earn, on average, 76 pence for every man's £1, and in the US, 77 cents for every man's $1, such reports are a 'highly selective and [an] ultimately misleading interpretation of pay data.' Average wages depend on ignoring differences such as employment type and total hours worked. The more that 'like for like' work is compared, the smaller the pay gap – and in some cases the pay gap vanishes. Sheila Wild, formerly of the UK's Equality and Human Rights Commission, has said that 'the statistics on the gender pay-gap are so various and so nuanced that almost anyone can take anything out of it and say what they want.'

Measuring distances in total pay 'masks a multitude of variables,' according to Joanna Williams. 'Older workers who have built careers through numerous promotions often earn more than junior colleagues; people working part-time earn less in total each year than people working full-time, even though they may be paid more each hour; some jobs are handsomely rewarded, many others pay the minimum wage. An 'average' includes the pay of everyone, from a shop-worker to the CEO of a large corporation.

> 'When the wages of women and men working in the same jobs for the same number of hours, at the same level and for the same number of years, are compared, there is no pay gap at all. In fact, when we compare the pay of men and women in their twenties, no matter which way we measure the statistics, we find that women are the higher earners.'

That's good news, isn't it? It's just that later on, women often make other choices – women are more likely to work part-time than men (female GPs frequently make that choice for family reasons). In the UK, 41 per cent of women work part time compared to 11 per cent of men.

Are women keener on a work-life balance than on constant, unrelenting full-time work? If so, that might eventually lead to an average gender pay gap. There is a greater problem, of course, as already referred to – which is that inequality in general has increased in recent decades, and as a star footballer or the vice-president of a university have seen their earnings rocket, the pay of nurses, care workers and those in the 'gig economy' seems so under-rewarded. Perhaps we pay for fluidity of work with insecurity of income. And this can apply to both mothers and fathers.

Gender theory

Judith Butler is an important name in the landscape of feminist and gender theory: she might be said to be the guru of gender theory, one of the most influential thinkers in feminist education, and, via education, politics and media. She is the source of the extraordinary success of gender theory, which despite dissent from scientific thinkers like Steven Pinker, has gained ground everywhere, and is now embedded in law in countries such as Canada.

Butler's philosophy is laid out in her many (expensive and yet best-selling) books on the subject. Here is an outline of her thesis on *Undoing Gender*:

> 'Gender is the apparatus by which the production and normalisation of masculine and feminine take place along with the interstitial forms of hormonal, chromosomal, psychic and performative that gender assumes. To assume that gender always and exclusively means the matrix of "masculine" and "feminine" is precisely to miss the critical point that the production of that coherent binary is contingent, that it comes at a cost, and that those permutations of gender which do not fit the binary are as much a part of gender as its most normative instance.

Gender is the mechanism by which notions of masculine and feminine are produced and naturalised, but gender might very well be the apparatus by which such terms are deconstructed and denaturalised.'

It was once affirmed that 'sex' was biological, while 'gender' was social. This has been refigured. Gender is now deemed to be a matter of choice, and the important thing is that it shouldn't be binary – that is, either 'masculine' or feminine'.

It is necessary to know this, though it is not obligatory – yet – to agree with it.

An experienced GP, Dr Sue Turner in Cornwall, wrote to *The Times* of London to affirm significant differences in sexuality between men and women. These are her findings: 'When females achieve orgasm oxytocin is released. This is the so-called "bonding" hormone. In my experience of more than forty years as a GP, girls who treat sex as casual recreation subconsciously learn not to orgasm in order to avoid this. The result is often difficult later on with this when they move into committed relationships. In this respect I think the sexes are truly different and that pressure put on girls to behave in this way is wrong.'* Some may feel that this is not convincing evidence to establish gender/sex differences; others may feel it accords with their own experiences.

According to a Norwegian study headed by Professor Leif Kennair, more than a third of women (35 per cent) regret a one-night stand. Far fewer men entertained such regrets (20 per cent). Gender theory has gained enormous influence world-wide, but individuals may experience the world quite differently, and quite differently from each other.

*males also release this hormone during orgasm

Gloria Steinem

I interviewed Gloria Steinem – that iconic feminist – twice. The first time was in New York in 1967. I was working for 'Londoner's Diary' on the *Evening Standard* – a great job, but a diary interview amounted to a pocket profile of perhaps 200 words. And yet when I approached Gloria Steinem – who was already famous for having worked as a bunny girl at Playboy (so as to expose Hugh Hefner's nefarious empire and the dismaying attitude to women) – she was extremely nice in her response and wholly obliging. She turned up for lunch at some downtown restaurant which I'd been recommended – it was half-smart, half-hip – swathed in a stunning coat and her trademark Aviator sunglasses atop her flowing locks. I thought she was terribly beguiling and I was greatly in awe of her – she was in her early thirties; I was in my early twenties. She had this wonderful, tinkling laugh. She was a feminine feminist, with her pretty clothes and understated but attractive, make-up. The conversation ranged over the various inequities to which women were subject.

Thirty years passed, and I got to interview Ms Steinem again, for the *Daily Mail*, in London in the 1990s. By this time I felt more critical of her attitude to motherhood: she never seemed to have a good word to say about maternity. She seemed to see it as an affliction, something so often imposed on women – and causing the population explosion, to boot. She was thinner than she had been when young, and the image of the austere schoolmarm disapproving of the fruitfulness of ordinary womankind did come to mind. She told me she felt unmoved by babies in any shape or form – she felt a far greater sense of sympathy and shared humanity with the old. She still had the tinkling laugh, but it seemed to be less frequently deployed.

The post-feminist thinker Camille Paglia would accord with my sense that Steinem was not sympathetic to motherhood. 'The childless Gloria Steinem, who was unmarried until she was sixty-six, has never been sympathetic to the problems faced by women who want both children and a job. Stay-at-home moms have been arrogantly disdained by orthodox feminism [which has] elevated abortion to sacramental status.'

Gloria Steinem's own childhood was not easy: a negative view of the condition of motherhood might well have derived from that experience. Her father left home, and her mother, depressed, poor and mentally disturbed, struggled to cope. Through a combination of brains, luck, timing and ambition (and good looks, which are seldom a disadvantage), Gloria Steinem had a successful university career and then a successful career in journalism. Her dedication to the causes of peace, justice and equity were entirely sincere. She could coin a phrase – or spot and popularise a nifty, witty one, such as 'A woman needs a man like a fish needs a bicycle' (funny, though not necessarily true for most women), and 'If men got pregnant, abortion would be a sacrament', which she heard from an Irish female taxi driver in America.

Gloria Steinem became a symbol of feminism partly because she was consistently committed to the cause, generous to other women, and perhaps, according to her own account, because she was not a politician, and therefore in a stand-alone situation. She has not been without criticism from other feminists. Jessa Crispin, who writes for *The Guardian* and *The New York Times*, has called Steinem 'that banal, CIA-funded icon for white, middle-class women'. Camille Paglia claims that Steinem 'stole the spotlight' from Betty Friedan. Friedan, according to Paglia, brought Steinem into the movement 'because of her telegenic good looks' and because Gloria made feminism seem 'reasonable and unthreatening', at a time when Betty Friedan was worried that militant lesbians – whom she called 'the lavender menace' – would drive mainstream women away. Subsequently, Friedan herself was 'marginalised'.

Paglia describes Gloria Steinem as 'a tireless, peripatetic activist' who 'played the role of stern guardian of a victim-centred ideology that did not permit alternate viewpoints. Steinem's male-bashing was overt... Meanwhile, she kept from pubic view how vital a role men played in her private life in Manhattan. Steinem also unapologetically aligned feminism with partisan Democratic politics.' Steinem compared Paglia's main work to *Mein Kampf,* and said that Camille Paglia 'calling herself a feminist is sort of like a Nazi saying they're not anti-Semitic.'

Sisterhood is powerful, but neither all women nor all feminists think alike, and critical knives have been sharpened in the fray. So what? Disagreement is healthy.

Grandmothers

Carl Jung believed that grandmothers played a vital role in the development of the human species, supporting younger parents while they worked, helping out with childcare, and transmitting the deposit of knowledge and cultural values. Evolutionary psychologists tend to support this view of the useful role that grandparents, particularly grandmothers, played in advancing the survival, and development, of the species.

In Sheila Kitzinger's book, *Women as Mothers*, she concludes that many cultures accord high status to women as grandmothers – especially as you travel eastwards around the globe. From the Caucuses onwards, the grandmother is a figure of social seniority and respect.

An obstetrician once told me: 'No woman knows whether she really wants to be a mother until she is one.' I would suggest that many women don't know whether they want to be mothers until they are grandmothers. I have known women – my own mother included – who were bored by their own babies when young, but utterly smitten by their grandchildren. Babies can become fascinating to observe and experience in old age, because the development of the child is such a riveting phenomenon, especially when you have the reflective time to observe it (and the affection and charm of young children is extraordinarily rewarding).

But you cannot choose to be a grandmother (or grandparent). You can only accept the course of events gratefully – as my friend Tim Pat Coogan put it when congratulated on becoming a great-grandfather: 'Not my doing – I only put down an initial deposit'. For some women who would be wonderful grandmothers – and have duly put down the initial deposit – it just doesn't happen. For others, it is an unexpected bonus out of the blue.

The status of grandparent-hood is highly fulfilling, but its occurrence is passive. It cannot be your choice and it is not within your 'agency' to bring it about. You depend upon others to deliver it. In our age, it is the greatest breach of family etiquette to suggest it should hurry up and happen. It is thus a situation over which you have no control, and the feminist aspiration for control over lifestyle decisions, in this sphere, amounts to nought.

Harassment at No. 10 Downing Street (and elsewhere)

A friend of my late mother-in-law took a job, during the First World War, at No. 10 Downing Street, when David Lloyd George was prime minister. Lloyd George was a notorious philanderer, and quick to grope any woman when he got the chance. My mother-in-law's friend was one of those Englishwomen of fortitude, cut from the same cloth as the fearless memsahibs who trampled across Africa and India. She was apparently an attractive young woman, and Lloyd George duly put his hand rather intimately on her well-shaped bottom.

'Unhand me, Prime Minister!' she boomed out in ringing tones, for all to hear. 'What do you take me for?'

Overcome with embarrassment, he duly 'unhanded' her and apologised profusely. She never had any trouble with him again. Yes, she was upper-class and confident, but so was Harriet Harman, many decades on.

In 2017, the Labour Party politician Harriet Harman – an experienced and confident front-bencher who was for a time acting leader of the Labour Party – published a memoir in which she described certain episodes of sexual harassment in her own youth. As a politics student at York University in the 1970s, she claims that her tutor, one Professor T.V. Sathyamurthy, promised her a better degree (from a 2:2 grade to a 2:1) if she agreed to have sex with him. She was outraged, she wrote, and refused, but did not complain.

Then, when she worked as an articled clerk in a lawyers' office, again in the 1970s, she writes that a lawyer at the firm 'crept up behind her' and 'groped' her when she was on the phone to a client, causing her to 'scream'. In 1991, she was again the subject of predatory male attention while at a function in Wales for her colleague Peter Hain: while dancing with some fellow politico, she was 'groped horribly'. In no case did she complain at the time.

We are all entitled to write about our experiences and how we coped (or didn't) with unwelcome advances, but I admire and prefer the approach of the forthright Suffragette of 1917 than Harman's post-hoc damsel-in-distress lamentations.

Professor Sathyamurthy died in 1998, and was in no position to confirm or deny the claim, but his former wife described Harriet Harman's account 'fanciful and unfair'. Mrs Sathyamurthy said that her husband was given to jokes and japes, but would not have behaved dishonourably. Yet forever more, whenever his name is mentioned, a quick Google search will associate him with such unethical conduct.

I used to hear donnish chaps who kept women out of institutions with the dire warning that 'women are trouble!' (It was a phrase much favoured by the novelist Kingsley Amis.) I also used to hear men say – when I worked in an all-male ambience – that 'only tarts kiss and tell'. I do, of course, now wonder if that was a code to shut women up. And there were women who were too frightened to complain about unwanted attention.

Camilla Paglia's advice is that 'when men step out of line, women should deal with it on the spot. Most men are cowed by women! Any woman worth her salt should know how to deal with men and put them in their place. Women must demand respect, and over time they will get it.' If a man 'makes a vulgar remark about your breasts ... don't slink off and whimper. Deal with it. On the spot. Say "Shut up, you jerk! And crawl back to the barnyard where you belong!"' We're talking about minor gestures here, not serious assaults or misconduct.

Let's end on a parliamentary note: Shirley Williams recounts the story of a male MP in the House of Commons who would pinch the bottoms of female colleagues as they went to vote. Rather than tell the whips, the female MPs decided to wear their sharpest stiletto heels into the voting lobbies. 'Few things hurt more than a stiletto driven into the foot,' writes Baroness Williams. The next day, the man hobbled into the tearoom with a very sore foot, to be met by the women MPs' mock-concern. He claimed it was gout, but he did not re-offend!

Historical change: from the Vote to *Good Housekeeping*

Political attitudes swing back and forth over the generations, because one generation often reacts against the generation that went before.

This is illuminated by the politics of my mother and grandmother.

My grandmother was born in 1870 in Galway (my parents were old when I was born, and I was born in the 1940s, so we're stretching back over three centuries). She was a dedicated and high-minded schoolteacher and became interested in politics, joining Sinn Féin soon after it began in 1905. She was of the Suffragette generation, although Irish women of her milieu who became politicised tended to be more involved with the 'national question' than with the campaign for 'Votes for Women', which would have had, perhaps, more of a British focus. (The first woman to be elected to the House of Commons, Constance Markievicz, was a Sinn Féin representative who refused to take her seat in a British parliament. She would have called herself a feminist, but being an Irish nationalist was a greater priority.) But my schoolteacher grandmother was certainly politically engaged – and culturally serious too. She took an interest in politics all her life. Seriousness of attitude had been the hallmark of Victorian feminists. 'Frivolousness' was ill-regarded. The feminist reformers, from Florence Nightingale onwards, deplored the way in which women were encouraged to be vain, narcissistic, and concerned with their appearance and the latest fashions. For that generation, only actresses wore make-up (and for stage performers, it was part of their profession).

My mother, born in 1902, came of age in a world that would be utterly changed by the First World War. As a young woman in the 1920s, she embraced everything that the sober feminists of the previous generation had disdained: the cocktails, the make-up, the bobbed hair, the shortened skirts, the painted fingernails, the film stars – and the freedom to smoke cigarettes. Her mother's values seemed starchy and puritanical. The Jazz Age represented a much more glamorous kind of liberation.

I was shocked, as a teenager, to learn that my mother once said that she had never exercised her vote. She had scant interest in doing so – she once described politics as 'a cod' (an Irishism for 'a swindle'). My mother was culturally refined, but she was far more interested in the decorative arts, beauty, cuisine and language than politics of any kind.

It's inevitable that the generations reflect changed values and different perspectives. The world changes and a battle won may be soon be forgotten.

British feminists who had lived through the experience of winning the vote – finally awarded without qualification in 1928 – became sorely disappointed and critical of the generations that followed. Between 1930 and 1950, the fight for the vote was old hat, and it seemed to feminists that there was a 'slide backwards' into domesticity and the 'feminine', rather than the feminist.

Even by the end of the 1920s, after the vote was finally won, Vera Brittain wrote, disappointingly, that feminists were now perceived as 'spectacled, embittered women, disappointed, childless, dowdy and generally unloved.'

There was a sort of sexual revolution in the 1920s, which was not at all the same as a feminist movement, and in some ways was the direct opposite to it. Sex manuals became bestsellers, such as Havelock Ellis's *The Psychology of Sex*, Helena Wright's *The Sex Factor in Marriage*, and Isabel Emslie Hutton's *The Sex Technique in Marriage*. Marie Stopes's renowned manuel *Married Love* was an opening sally in the campaign for birth control, and it was emphatic about the importance of attaining sexual satisfaction. Theodore Van de Velde's *Ideal Marriage, its Physiology and Technique*, went through eight printings.

Many of these books emphasised not only the joy of sex, but undermined or even attacked women who were not happily paired up in wedlock. 'Frigidity' in women was anathemised. 'Spinsterhood' was almost pathologised. The psychologist Janet Chance deplored the effect of 'spinster politicians, whether unmarried or single' (implying that if married, they must be 'frigid'). Susan Kingsley Kent has written that feminists, by the 1930s, were 'seen as abnormal, sexually maladjusted women who hated men'. The Jazz generation wanted none of that old, high-minded stuff.

And then along came the cosmetics revolution – with Mesdames Helena Rubinstein and Elizabeth Arden leading the field of globally marketing make-up for all women. Feminists like Lady Rhonda (who ran the magazine, *Time and Tide*: she was herself lesbian – it was nicknamed *Sappho's*

Weekly in journalistic circles) were horrified at the way in which cosmetics were taking over the popular women's magazines.

Magazines such as *Good Housekeeping, Woman's Own, Woman's Illustrated, Woman, My Weekly, Home Chat,* and *Woman and Home* began to acquire huge circulations in the 1930s (*Woman* sold 750,000 copies in 1937, and would have three and a half million copies sold by the 1950s), and the formula was, across the board, the same: how to get (and satisfy) a husband, and how to embellish a home (*Good Housekeeping* increased the domestic burden on women by advocating high standards in good housekeeping).

The aspiration that women's only goals were a fulfilling marriage and maintaining an ideal home lasted until the 1950s, which was just about when my generation was growing up. And in our turn, we reacted against the definitions of womanhood which had prevailed, internationally, since the late 1920s. And thus the Women's Liberation Movement of the 1960s began.

Housework and inequality

A Canadian academic, Dr Stephen Marche, maintains that one of the reasons why women have not attained full equality with men is that they fuss too much about cleaning the house. You can't pursue real achievement if you're worried about scouring the cooker. My sentiments precisely. But don't underestimate the social pressure – ever – to be a good housewife. As a slap-dash housewife – I more or less do my best but I resent too much time spent on household chores – I think I can claim victim status on that count. People make subtle remarks, don't you know, about one's low standards of housewifery. (A neighbour once brought me an artificial flower on moving house: 'I know you'd never take care of a real plant.') This is a fact: people will judge a woman for being a bit of a slob, and it's the fear of being judged that drives many of us on to do a bit of a household blitzing from time to time, when, according to Dr Marche, we might be spending time getting ahead instead.

Germaine Greer is dismissive of housework. 'A housewife's work has no results. It simply has to be done again.' Simone de Beauvoir claims that time spent in the kitchen reinforces 'passivity', 'acceptance', and even, perhaps, 'submission' in women. 'Each day the kitchen ... teaches [the housewife] patience and passivity; here is alchemy; one must obey the fire, the water, wait for the sugar to melt, for the dough to rise, and also for the wash to dry, for the fruits to ripen on the shelf.' And there are aspects of kitchen and home management which refuse to be controlled: 'There are materials that will stand washing and others that persist, objects that break all by themselves, dust that springs up like plants.' De Beauvoir has little time for the patience of the gardener, either, who falls in with the cycle of the seasons: all this generates more feminine passivity: 'Woman's mentality perpetuates that of agricultural civilisations which worshipped the magic powers of the land; she believes in magic.'

This is all a bit fanciful: those celebrity chefs and cooks we see on TV tend to be dynamos of active egomania rather than magic-believing passive creatures waiting upon the alchemy of nature and time. And when you visit a perfectly ordered home, in which everything is wonderfully well-arranged and kept clean and tidy, you do, often, think better of the person who ordered it, woman or man. Sometimes I pass houses on the street where I live, and see in through their front windows, admiring the domestic arts that make them look so inviting, cosy, pretty and comfortable: where the dedicated investment in a home is clearly evident.

Earlier feminists sometimes contrasted the useful and fulfilled lives of busy housewives (like Mrs Pepys) with the frustrating and pointless existence of 'ladies' who felt imprisoned by the want of occupation.

Yet everything in life is a matter of priorities. If you prioritise one aspect of your time, it diminishes another. Stephen Marche claims that men achieve more because, for the most part, they don't give a damn whether the household chores are done or not; that's not true of all men, but it is often true of men who put a greater priority on something other than getting through the daily list of household chores. This is also true of women – but women are more likely to feel the stigma (from others or themselves) of being slobs.

Imperialism

Imperialism and colonialism are not ideas that find much favour in our time: you can't go off and start taking over someone else's country. Fair point.

But imperialism and colonialism did sometimes bring benefits to women. The British Raj put a stop to *suttee* in India (whereby a widow was expected to throw herself on her husband's burning pyre at his funeral – quite an incentive to keep a guy alive!), and 'honour killings' in part of the sub-continent that became Pakistan (when young women were killed by their brothers if they 'dishonoured' the family by an alleged lack of decorum).

In China, the British (and Irish) missionaries did their best to halt foot-binding, which continued well into the 1900s: the feet of girls were bound tightly, so that all their lives, women would hobble on tiny, weak, girlish feet.

In Africa, polygamy was discouraged by British and French influences. This is now seen as meddling with indigeonous practices, and perhaps it was. But it probably does enhance the status of women to be the only wife, rather than one amongst many.

Under imperial rule, education for girls was also made more widely available. In India, a convent education came to be regarded as a status symbol, because it apparently imparted an element of 'refinement'. But it also imparted education.

Germaine Greer has said that 'if Irish nuns hadn't tramped across the broiling Australian desert' in the nineteenth century, many Australian women would never have had an education.

Irish Women's Liberation Movement

At some point each year, a small group of now elderly Irish women meet in Dublin for what dear Nell McCafferty calls 'the Dying Feminists' Lunch'. Some of the group who together founded the Irish Women's Liberation Movement in 1970 have now passed on to their eternal reward (as the Irish saying once had it). June Levine died from a stroke; Mary Anderson from breast cancer; Mary McCutcheon, most tragically of all, as a young mother, with her twin babies, in a car accident; Nuala Fennell, who became a successful parliamentarian and government minister, of heart failure after valiantly living with a blood disorder for some years; Mary Cummins died of lung cancer in her late fifties – but an annual Women in Media festival is held in her memory in her native Ballybunion. One of the older members who helped found the movement, Margaret Gaj, lived to a ripe old age, but has also died.

There's a standard history of the IWLM, written by an American, Anne Stopper, which diligently recounts the story of what she calls a 'formidable' accomplishment that had a strong impact on the changes that followed (or were already underway) in Irish society. The IWLM somehow jelled and brought together a dynamic group of mostly young women, from varying backgrounds, all drawn to what was then termed 'Women's Liberation'. We produced a succinct and quite hard-hitting short book, *Chains or Change*, now, astonishingly, considered to be a historic document (available in the National Library of Ireland: my own copy has gone with my archives to Dublin City University). *Chains or Change* is in some ways a revolutionary model: it looks for larger change, and yet spells out specific goals. Its demands seem achievable. Either by instinct or by judgement, it did not make demands which the market wouldn't bear: it scarcely mentioned divorce (wise, since married women's property rights at the time were not secure enough to extend financial protection after divorce), and it didn't mention abortion – it was far more important to bring about a change in the 1935 law which prohibited contraception (or 'birth control artefacts'). I don't even remember any mention of abortion rights in our discussions: it was just a bridge too far for most Irish women at the time. I saw the letters sent to me as woman's editor of a national newspaper, the *Irish Press*: many came from rural women in the west of Ireland who felt downtrodden and oppressed by laws and practices – but these were also Irish mothers who adhered to their faith and family. In any realistic movement, you have to take people with you, not insult their values.

This is the roll-call of names mentioned by Anne Stopper in her chronicle: Mary Anderson, Mary Cummins, Mairin de Burca, Mary Holland, Maureen Johnston, Mary Kenny, Mary Maher, Mary McCutcheon, Marie McMahon, Mary Robinson (nee Bourke), Mary Sheerin, Moira Woods: and, of course, just as significantly, Eavan Boland, Margaret Gaj, Elgy Gillespie, June Levine, Nell McCafferty, Margaret MacCurtain – who, by the way, was and is a Dominican nun – Finnuala O'Connor, Eimer Philbin Bowman and Rosita Sweetman. (I would also add the names of Mavis Arnold, Colette O'Neill and Bernadette Quinn.) Please notice how many of these Irish women's liberationists had baptismal names of 'Mary' (Maureen, and the Irish language version, 'Mairin', means 'Little Mary'). I'd be surprised if many of the rest of the group didn't have Mary as a middle name. Ireland was a Marian country, and Mary, the Mother of Jesus, was historically often called the Queen of Ireland.

It was a spirited group – left, right and centre – and I won't say there weren't tensions within the group, because there always are, but tensions can add energy. The left always brings a kind of dynamic – a driven understanding of Marxism, and a gritty commitment to direct action – and the right reassures the middle-classes (whose support is vital) that change and reform are rational and sensible. The left demanded action on housing (we're still waiting for that, you could say – housing needs are chronic in Dublin), but everyone supported equal pay, the demolition of the marriage bar (in State and semi-State bodies, women were obliged to resign from their job when they married), welfare support for single mothers and deserted wives (they had none at the time), the entitlement to serve on juries (abolished by the Irish Free State in 1927 – admittedly because so many women asked to be excused), and equal financial status (women had to obtain the counter-signature of a man to open a credit account, and in some cases, to open a bank account).

It was contraception rights that hit the headlines, being, in every sense of the word, 'sexier', and it was altogether sensational when we took a train between Dublin and Belfast, obtained a handful of condoms and spermicides, and brought these illegal items back over the Irish border, declaring them at Dublin's Connolly Station. I have written elsewhere about my own version of this event, so I won't repeat the narrative. I'll just say, in short, it was a stunt that made an impact, being just shocking enough to bring some disapproval, and just provocative enough to cause excitement, and a kind of piquant enjoyment by proxy – people who don't want to do outrageous things themselves like to vicariously enjoy others doing so.

The media loved it and we were very adept in using the media. A musical has since been composed and performed around this episode, entitled, *The Train*, though I have deliberately stayed away from attending a performance. I'm too nervous that I might shout out 'that's not the way it was!' and spoil everyone's evening. I was irked when a woman at a Cork literary event told me that what she liked best about *The Train* was 'the bit about substituting aspirins for contraceptive pills – great fun!' The contraceptive pill was never banned in the Republic of Ireland since it hadn't been invented in 1935, and you cannot ask to be arrested for 'illegal importations' if what you are declaring is actually legal. I'm a bit crabby and pedantic about historical points of information.

But the mass meeting at the Mansion House in Dublin on 14 April 1971 was probably far more significant. Nell McCafferty, a passionate and eloquent orator, spoke to a packed chamber about the aims and meaning of the IWLM, and the effect was stunning. Marie McMahon told Anne Stopper: 'The Mansion House to me would have been the equivalent of the Russian Revolution. We had succeeded in raising awareness and we had organised this marvelous, fantastic meeting and every woman at that meeting was a raging inferno of anger and frustration.' But also, I think, elation: the IWLM had launched a new wave of feminism in Ireland.

In later years, life's journey took us in different directions: a disparate group can only hang together for a short, immediate campaign. Looking back, I do not disavow the ideals of the Irish Women's Liberation Movement, and I'm sometimes stopped in the street, or at an event, or at a theatre, by women who says 'thank you for changing life for women in Ireland'. That's kind, but life, I think, would have changed anyway. The IWLM was, in essence, a modernising movement: Ireland needed to catch up with the social changes that were happening since the Second World War (Éire's neutrality at that time had a 'sealing' effect on society). Many of the conditions that we sought to change had been obtained in other European countries since the 1940s – we were just a generation behind. What do we talk about at the Dying Feminists' Lunch? Mostly, I think, good memories.

Jokes and anecdotes in the battle of the sexes

- A male definition of an ideal woman: 'A deaf and dumb nymphomaniac who lives over a pub.' The charming, gentle and much-loved television personality and humourist Frank Muir once cited this as an example of laddish humour. I have it on the authority of his son-in-law that he always continued to find this comical, and so it is. It would not be permitted in the public realm today, because it appears so misogynistic. But it is not all that it seems. In a way, it is a joke against the teller, as it conjures up a dim Neanderthal of a male who thinks a silent and compliant woman, aided by easy access to alcohol, is some kind of ideal. Every woman to whom I have told this joked has laughed heartily.
- An Irishman is walking along a country road when he spots a bottle gleaming by the wayside. He picks up the bottle and opens it, and out comes a benign genie.

The genie says to him: 'This is your lucky day. I can grant you a wish. You can have anything that is in my power.'

The Irishman replies: 'Anything I like? That's wonderful! Well, what I really want is a highway from my home on the west coast of Ireland all the way to New York, so that I can drive to see the bright lights of Manhattan and enjoy the wonders of Broadway whenever I want, because I hate flying. A transatlantic bridge from my front door to Times Square would do me just fine!'

The genie's brow furrowed in consternation. 'Oh, come on, be reasonable – that's not what I mean,' he replied testily. 'No one has ever managed to build a bridge of that length – completely new technology would be required to cope with the movement of the earth's tectonic plates, you've got the Mid-Atlantic trench miles deep, and there are those vast icebergs that would wreck the bridge in spring, plus the likelihood of hurricanes moving up from Florida… Please – something within reason.'

'Oh,' says the Irishman, disappointed. 'A different wish then. You know, when I look at my wife working about the house, I have absolutely no idea what's going on in her head. Please – give me the power to read a woman's thoughts.'

The genie reflected for a moment or two, and came back with another idea. 'That transatlantic highway – do you want it two-lane or four?'

- Dorothy Parker was one of the few people to joke about abortion. When she became pregnant by a handsome-looking cad (she had a weakness for the type), she jested, after a termination: 'Trust me to put all my eggs in one bastard.' But the joke contained pain just the same.
- There's an old Hollywood joke which goes: 'Did you hear about the starlet who was so dim she slept with the writer?' The screenwriter was always the lowest man on the totem pole (as Scott Fitzgerald found). This, apparently, has now changed, with the success of *Mad Men*, *Breaking Bad* and *The Crown*. And the expectation that the starlet has to wend her way by sexual favours

is questioned at least by Hollywood actresses/female-actors.

- A Russian male with whom I fell into conversation on a train journey said to me, somewhat lugubriously (in a heavy Russian accent): 'There is no such thing as an unattractive woman. There is only not enough vodka.'

Kinships

(1) The mothers of sons

A young woman is about to go into labour and give birth. She and her partner have chosen not to be told whether their baby will be a boy or a girl: they want it to be a surprise. The onset of labour begins – those of us who have been through it remember that moment when you become aware you are possessed by a force of nature that can be helped or ameliorated (fortunately), but not resisted. And at last, the infant is born – and it's a boy.

Now she is the mother of a son. She may become the mother of a daughter in the future, but if she is a feminist, her perspective of the world will subtly, or perhaps even affirmatively, shift as she begins to see life through the prism of his experience. She may come to feel, as the feminist Angela Phillips did, that raising a boy requires some special applications – who would later write a book about it, called *The Trouble With Boys*. I began to feel, myself, that one of the reasons why traditional lore counsels 'little boys shouldn't cry' is because they seem, sometimes, to cry rather more than little girls. Little girls – and I'm generalising here, but the thought occurs – often seem more robust, more self-confident, quicker to learn, quicker to potty-train, quicker with language and interpersonal skills. In their teenage years, boys seem lumpen adolescents while girls of the same age seem self-possessed young women.

The mother of a son will sometimes rephrase Tammy Wynette's lyrics, reflecting that, 'Sometimes it's hard to be a man.'

The mothers of sons read, apprehensively, about how much more frequent suicide is among young men than among young women.

The mothers of sons express their dissatisfaction that boys are falling behind in school studies (and universities) because teachers and academics are now favouring girls (it is claimed).

When there's a rape or sexual assault case in the public realm, the mothers of sons may feel that it is unfair that an accused male can be named, and thus forever shamed, even if found innocent, while a female accuser may be protected by anonymity, even if her claim is false.

And if a son's marriage should be dissolved, his mother may well feel that her ex-daughter-in-law has taken her son to the cleaners, financially, and withholds or manipulates custody of the children. Oh, yes, I've listened to all those accounts from the mothers of sons.

There are older mothers who feel that men are disadvantaged in marriage, in divorce, and as fathers. Some of these older women were, themselves, once young feminists. But being the mothers of sons has made them see things from the other end of the telescope.

(2) The daughters of fathers

When Margaret Thatcher was in primary school, she won a class prize, and was congratulated by a visiting relative.

'You're a lucky little girl,' she was told. But little Maggie was having none of it. 'I'm not lucky – I deserved it,' retorted the moppet. Good attitude, too!

But where did she get that confidence – the daughter of a Lincolnshire grocer and his demure, Methodist wife? From her father, who had every confidence in her from the moment she was born. An affirming father is one of the best gifts a young girl can have, and there are many studies which reflect this, and many examples of confident and high-achieving women who get that sense of worth from their fathers. Indira Gandhi was her father's closest companion and political heir. The military painter, Lady Butler, who experienced sensational artistic success in the 1870s at a time when women were not even admitted to the Royal Academy – was tirelessly encouraged and advanced by her father.

It's no coincidence that the most accomplished female film director to emerge in Hollywood in recent years is Sofia Ford Coppola – very much her father's daughter. I wasn't surprised to discover that one of Britain's foremost intellectuals, Professor Lisa Jardine, was the daughter of Jacob Bronowski, the brilliant mathematician and author of *The Ascent of Man*. Dame Anna Wintour, world queen of the fashion industry – editor of American *Vogue*, as portrayed by Meryl Streep in *The Devil Wears Prada* – was adored, encouraged and idolised by her father, Charles Wintour, my first newspaper editor, who I came to know very well. He thought Anna was the greatest genius since Leonardo da Vinci.

The only woman in history who has taken charge of the Vatican was Lucrezia Borgia. Her father, Pope Alexander VI – Roderigo Borgia – had full confidence in his daughter and turned over the entire administration of the Holy See to her when he had to be absent. When Ivanka Trump took her father's seat at the G20 table in 2017, I thought it a neat parallel.

I think I can spot the inner confidence of a woman who has had an encouraging father. A study by Jennifer Mascaro and James Rilling at Emory University in Georgia found that fathers 'pay more attention' to their daughters than their sons, starting from early childhood. These, of course, are the good fathers.

And I think I can detect, also, where a father was inadequate, abusive, absent or abandoning. Many feminists, in my experience, had absent or inadequate fathers – the psychological hole left by poor fathering is exactly what drove their discontent.

Language issues

A somewhat old-fashioned British parliamentarian, Sir Roger Gale (Tory, aged seventy-three), got into hot water for describing the women who work with him at the House of Commons – including his wife – as 'girls'. An order went out from on high to disbar MPs from employing their family members as assistants, researchers and secretaries, and Sir Roger's wife, Suzy, who had run his parliamentary office for thirty-four years, thought such a ban was utterly ridiculous. She had been an experienced press officer in a parliamentary constituency when she first met her husband, and working together subsequently enabled her to mesh her personal and work life harmoniously – as spouse and mother – and, thank you very much, she did the job jolly well.

Her husband then added that 'all the girls' in his office enjoyed their work with him.

At this use of 'girls', an explosion of protest followed. How dare he patronise grown women as 'girls'? That was wrong, patriarchal language. Dr B. J. Epstein, feminist and senior lecturer at the University of East Anglia, said that describing women as 'girls' in this way was disrespectful, 'amounted to subjugation', and treated them effectively as children. Debi Hill, one of the 'girls' – aged forty-seven – and the MP's office manager said she didn't mind a bit.

Focusing on substance rather than style, Ms Hill added that 'We feel very valued, very appreciated' at work.

Where language is concerned, the person who is the object is the one most entitled to make a judgement. If Ms Hill did not object to being called a 'girl', then it's her call.

These matters are, in the end, personal, and we all have our personal preferences. I would have no objection to being described as a girl: but I loathe being called 'darlin'', 'my love', and even 'my lovely' by strangers who are quite simply patronising me as an older woman. (If the next person in line is a man, they usually address him as 'sir'.)

However, as with many factors, there could also be a class issue. I have a close friend who mixes in rather more upper-class circles, and she never gets addressed as 'darlin'' by perfect strangers. But I suppose that's the difference between shopping at Fortnum & Mason and the local M&S.

The spat over Sir Roger Gale's language rather obscured the original issue – the banning of family members from working with parliamentarians. Suzy Gale is surely right: it's almost a definition of a 'family-friendly' work policy for which so many feminists have been striving for so long. Banning the practice would very likely be to the disadvantage of women.

Lingo misogyny

The late Bernard Levin thought himself very wise and wonderful when he delivered this adage to me, comparing translations of texts – novels, poetry, the lyrics of operas – to the character of women.

'*Les traductions sont comme les femmes: quand elles sont belles, elles ne sont pas fideles/ Quand elles sont fideles, elles ne sont pas belles.*' That is: 'Translations are like women: when they are beautiful, they're not faithful, and when they're faithful, they're not beautiful.' (In translating the observation, it has been indeed rendered less mellifluous.)

What a mean thing to say – that women who are beautiful are seldom faithful! But I learned something more informative when I did a module on translation while pursuing a French degree. Translation can be faithful where the translator is skilled, and understands that where there is loss of nuance in the original text, there must be compensation. That's the key to translation: there is loss, and there is compensation. A much more interesting observation about texts, and even about life.

As it happens, by the way, we are living in an era of brilliant women translators. Anthea Bell, who translates from the French and the German, is something akin to a genius – she renders the puns in *Asterix* from French to English quite peerlessly. Having read both versions of

Asterix, I would say that Anthea Bell's translations are both beautiful and faithful.

There are many very distinguished and award-winning women translators at work today: Margaret Jull Costa, Deborah Smith – from the Korean – Megan McDowell, Eyvor Fogarty (from the Hungarian and Russian). An especially admirable translator is Mary Hobson, a novelist and mother of four who began studying Russian at the age of fifty-six, started going to university at the age of sixty-two, and became, in her sixties, a prize-winning translator from the Russian, especially the works of Alexander Pushkin, a great Russian writer.

Mansplaining

Mansplaining: *verb; informal. Gerund or present participle: (of a man) explain (something) to someone, typically a woman, in a manner regarded as condescending or patronising.*

Personally, I like people explaining things to me, and I don't mind if it's a man or a woman. If a man knows a lot about particle physics, then I'd like it explained. I would have loved to have had some brilliant mentor, male or female, who explained a lot of things to me (instead of having to find out everything for myself, blundering through life).

The main thing is that the person who is doing the explaining should know what they're talking about. I'm a bit less receptive to younger people explaining facts to me that I discovered fifty years ago. Then I remind myself what a news editor once told me: 'Remember, every time Beethoven's Fifth Symphony is played, someone is hearing it for the first time.' Old knowledge is always new to someone.

Nobody likes being patronised, to be sure. I remember being furious when a (male) consultant obstetrician told me, during a pregnancy concern: 'Don't worry your pretty little head about it. We know how to bring babies into the world.' I was about to feel enraged as a woman, when he followed it up with the quip: 'I know a lot about Ireland. I come from the capital of Ireland myself – Liverpool. Ha, ha!' Some folk are just prattish – you can't let it affect your blood pressure.

Younger women feel patronised by 'mansplaining'. So do some older people. 'Mansplaining is utterly rife in this country,' wrote Natasha Ogilivie to *The Oldie* magazine, 'and as I get older it becomes more common. I am treated like an idiot by mid-level male executives who assume I'm just a little woman who has obviously done nothing with her life. As a working woman I would have had the power to hire and fire them!'

I think this is why older women are sometimes bossy. They have to be.

Manspreading

One of the current tactics for putting manners on menfolk has been to prohibit 'manspreading' – that is, men sitting on public transport with their legs and posteriors taking up more public space than their fair share.

Madrid's left-wing city authority erected public signs that warned male passengers against this offence. Honestly, this is what the fierce old Spanish socialist movement has come to – teaching etiquette rules to uncouth blokes on public transport! Dolores Ibarruri – 'La Pasionaria' – who fierily led the Spanish left with the ringing words, 'It's better to die on your feet than to live on your knees,' is well and truly mocked by the Miss Manners instructions that it's better to keep your knees together, chaps.

It's patently selfish to take up more than your allotted space on public transport, but it's hardly a burning political or civic issue. In any case, obese people of either gender are apt to take up more space than they might.

Public transport authorities are entitled to ask all passengers to show common consideration for others. And if so, they should also enforce such regulations. Travelling on Irish Rail, I hear constant reminders over the public address system to 'keep feet off seats'. Despite that, there were always some uncouth youths – of either gender – who prop up their shoes, fresh from street dust and dog dirt, on the opposing seats, and no one dares to correct them.

Putting your street shoes on the seats is a rather more unhygienic practice than 'manspreading', so before 'manspreading' is taken up by every city authority in Europe, I'd prefer if travel authorities would enforce their regulations on the former. But then virtue signalling is often preferred to practical action.

Market values

Notice on a hairdressing salon window in North London:

'Hairstyles: Women: cut and blow-dry: £45. Men: cut and finish: £20.'

Does the difference occur because women more often have longer hair? No, because it is not predicated on the length of hair; and anyway, some women have hair as short as many men, but the tariff is not reduced thereby.

The inequality here lies with the essence of market capitalism. For some commodities the price of anything is the price a customer will pay for it. How much is a Picasso, a Basquiat, a Damien Hirst? How much is a telephone apparatus that Hitler once used? How much is it to hire a lawyer to supervise your will (varies enormously)?

Since the price of many commodities and services is the price that a buyer is prepared to pay, the question any retailer or service provider will address is: 'What will the market bear?'

The hairdressing salon is supposing that women will pay more to have their hair coiffed. The supposition is probably correct. The test will be whether the salon stays in business.

The hairdressing price, by the way, also stipulates 'Monday to Friday'. Presumably, the cost is greater on a Saturday because there is more weekend demand.

Socialist societies have tried to correct the market mechanism, and some societies with a strong commitment to social equality have had some success in some areas. There is a reasonable argument for statutory price controls on certain public utilities – the gas company and the water board should not, perhaps, be permitted to charge whatever they think will serve their employees or shareholders best.

But in commodities and in services, it's very difficult to avoid the iron laws of demand and supply: a hotel that is empty may charge £100 for a room: a hotel that is almost full may charge £600 for the same room. Where there is strong control and regulation of demand and supply, a black market usually springs up. Sweden discourages alcohol abuse by making liquor very expensive: but there are reckoned to be 35,000 illegal stills in the country manufacturing moonshine, and selling at a price that the market will bear.

The film actress Sienna Miller, complaining that Hollywood has often under-paid female talent quite unfairly – the gap has often been 'staggering', she says – has suggested that in the film business, an actress (or female actor, if you prefer) should routinely be paid more. 'You're so leaned on as a woman to promote a film by doing magazine covers, by what you wear on red carpets … they rely on that so heavily that you really should be compensated sometimes more than your male co-stars for what you're asked to do.' According to Sienna, women's acceptance of unequal payment is because 'it's part of what you accept and tolerate as a woman, because you have a deep-rooted inferiority.'

But Hollywood, too, probably conforms to the law of supply and demand. There are any number of beautiful young women who seek to be film stars, and who will often do almost anything to become film stars: so the supply is copious and greatly outstrips the places available. There are legions of beautiful young women who are happy to be photographed on red carpets and appear on magazine covers without any remuneration at all.

Maybe Sienna could launch a trade union that would regulate matters more favourably?

There's another market law which we veterans of the market-place have long known: when you're hot, you're hot, and you can command big bucks. When you're not hot, you're glad of any work at all. That's the way it works. I admire any feminist who tries to change it. Capitalism is a lot tougher to crack than it looks.

Some market changes are in our own hands. Women regularly pay more for toiletries and cosmetics than men, for no very good reason except that the retailers believe that women will pay more. A man's fragrance will cost 20 per cent less than a woman's – so choose that nice lemoney aftershave rather than the prettily-packaged feminine toilet water. If you want to shave your legs, purchase a man's cheaper razor rather than the more expensive 'ladyshave' pitched at the female market, and priced accordingly. And if you want equal costs at the coiffeur, ask for the chap's price at the local barber.

Marriage

'Marriage is the destiny traditionally offered to women by society. It is still true that most women are married, or have been, or plan to be, or suffer from not being.'
Simone de Beauvoir, *The Second Sex*

Feminism has often regarded marriage ambiguously. Often, it was pointed out that women were disadvantaged by becoming wives: spinsters and widows enjoyed civil equality and social independence, but wives were often under the control of husbands, and enjoyed fewer rights. Rape was not recognised as an assault within marriage until recently. A husband was responsible for his wife's debts, as though she were too infantile to take responsibility herself. Marriage arose from patriarchy and women were regarded as chattels: the practice of a father 'giving away' a bride in a wedding ceremony alluded to a woman being transferred from her father's responsibility to her husband's.

De Beauvoir and Germaine Greer also greatly disapprove of the way that young women are taught to 'please' men in the hope of obtaining a husband: this was another form of oppression. Greer raged against the way in which women were constantly taught to smile, the better to please, to cajole, to charm. This was the conduct of an underling.

Marriage, in Ireland, was not always upheld as a natural or inevitable destiny. After the Great Famine of 1845–52, the Irish became notoriously reluctant to marry, and turned to a prudent celibacy in droves (which the Catholic religion facilitated – monasticism had historically been far more admired than conjugality). In the 1950s, about a quarter of Irish people did not marry at all, which was considered to be exceptionally high. Social observers from overseas frequently remarked on the 'extreme prudence' with which the Irish peasant viewed wedlock. As a young girl, it was never – that I can recall – suggested to me that I should look for (or even hope for) a husband: the nuns at my convent school were themselves consecrated virgins and husbands were not really on their agenda. In my home life, I received the impression that since good husbands were rather difficult to obtain, a girl of my modest gifts shouldn't perhaps rely upon it as an option. The standard for marriage, in accordance with the Irish reluctance to marry, seemed to be rather high. My sister, who was prettier and had a better figure, was thought to have a better chance in the marriage market.

Marriage was, first of all, for those who could afford it (the Irish caution towards marriage was often economic – you couldn't marry until you could afford to support a family). Some women, particularly in farming areas, might have attractive dowries that made them measurably more marriageable. Some women came from high-status families – their society photographs would appear in *Irish Tatler & Sketch* – where they would be highlighted as sought-after as brides. And some women were very accomplished home-makers, which increased their value. I had an aunt, on my father's side, who really was quite plain to look at, yet married a wealthy and successful man. When questioned about the dynamics of this, my mother said of her sister-in-law: 'She is a wonderful home-maker. Marvellous taste. Great cook. Runs the house flawlessly.' It was a big house, too, on the magnificent Vico Road in Dalkey, Co. Dublin.

A neighbouring spinster, by contrast, once told me that I would certainly never 'get' a husband if I couldn't make curtains. Or build a successful fire in the hearth – my attempts seemed to always result in a smoke-filled room.

The American feminists I read in the 1960s and 1970s railed strongly against the tyranny of marriage – because America was a high-marriage society, and popular culture did indeed urge every young woman to marry, and to marry young. Even for Helen Gurley Brown, in her groundbreaking (and emphatically mercenary) publication, *Sex and the Single Girl*, first published in 1962, the ultimate prize was to capture a man and nail him down.

American feminists tended to proclaim that their oppression lay in the fact that there was really 'no other choice' for women but to marry. It wasn't entirely true, but America certainly was, until the end of the twentieth century, a high-marriage society. But this was not a universal condition.

Is marriage a tyranny? It can be. So can the alternative.

Marriage: gay and straight

Back in those 'summer of love' epochs of the 1960s, the accepted view among progressive persons was that marriage was (1) a patriarchal repressive institution, just as Engels said, invented by men to control women, property and the legitimacy of offspring; (2) a meaningless piece of paper which had nothing to do with the authenticity of a relationship. When couples married, they usually said it was just for tax reasons. Tax reasons, indeed, figured quite high on the agenda among progressive liberals. When I married on 25 March, our left-wing friends cried out in protest: 'You're crazy! It's the end of the tax-year!' To wait another week or so would have made much more sense, but it seemed too much trouble to change the arrangement. However, I did learn from this that fiscal advantages do matter when it comes to wedlock. I have observed, even more acutely, couples who affirmed the joys of living together – rather than subjecting themselves to a patriarchal, oppressive institution invented to control women – nonetheless tend to marry quietly in later life, since inheritance law can be a right mess if this path is not taken.

The theory that marriage is an oppressive, patriarchal institution is at variance with the evidence that, historically, it so often seemed to be women who were keen on wedlock, and men who seemed to dodge it. A close reading of the agony-aunt pages often revealed this theme, and the ongoing complaints of young women in their thirties about males who 'won't commit' tends to repeat the motif. The smokey-voiced Mariella Frostrup has alluded to this experience – all the chaps she knew who were ready to have fun, but not to 'settle down'.

As already mentioned, the late Helen Gurley Brown (the founder of the modern version of *Cosmopolitan* magazine), wrote *Sex and the Single Girl* in 1962. The title sounded liberating, but the underlying purpose of the book was the pursuit of a man to 'catch' and keep as a remedy against age and loneliness. Make the best of your single years, HGB urged: 'During your best years, you don't need a husband … marriage is an insurance for the worst years of your life.' In your pursuit of a man, open a file on the men you know but eliminate the undesirables and the losers: 'The weirdies, creepies, dullies, snobs, hopeless neurotics and mamas' darlings.' Have no truck with unemployed men – regard them as 'untouchables'. And avoid any man with sex problems. 'Him you don't need.'

HGB insists that there's nothing wrong with having a married man as a lover – though a girl must insist 'he brings her presents' and pays for treats – but as they probably won't leave their wives, they may not be husband material.

Ruthlessly searching for a man 'for insurance against your worst years' is hardly in alignment with the view that the whole set-up is just a patriarchal conspiracy to oppress women, even if the Women's Movement of the 1960s did come to regard marriage as little better than prostitution. Some Women's Liberation texts of this period extol prostitution as more honest than marriage: the prostitute only sells her body by the hour and can change the deal whenever she chooses, whereas the wife has sold herself into wedlock 'till death us do part'.

Marriage ground-rules changed somewhat over the years that followed: legislatures ruled that rape was not permissible in marriage (previously, it was held that a man could not rape his wife, since conjugal rights were implicit): property and pension rights for women were enhanced. Wedlock became more equal – so equal that a men's movement arose to protest against the unfair treatment of males in divorce settlements and child custody cases.

And then along came gay marriage, a movement that emerged with surprising alacrity in the late 1990s, and won hearts and minds all over the western world within twenty-five years of its inception. Thousands of years of human development, in which marriage was universally deemed as a contract between a man and a woman, with a view to enhancing a dynasty, were overturned with quite amazing speed. In 2016, the Republic of Ireland became the first country to vote for same-sex marriage by public referendum.

In the wake of gay marriage, we heard no more about wedlock being a horrible oppressive institution invented for the purposes of patriarchal oppression: suddenly, marriage was about 'the right to love' who you chose: the entitlement to have your conjugal partnership celebrated, acknowledged and recognised in law. Suddenly, marriage was something absolutely wonderful, and to deny it was a barbarous and inhumane attitude. And *The Times* indeed reported that the introduction of gay marriage had bumped up the marriage statistics.

It's funny how things turn out. Some of the attitudes to wedlock embraced by feminists in the 1960s and 70s have been undermined and even dissolved by the rise of gay marriage, which has reclaimed, with a grand flourish, matrimony as a romantic ideal – a lifelong, loving commitment to one spouse, forsaking all others. Elton John and David Furnish have even reinstated the word 'husband', just as the Irish politician Katherine Zappone and her spouse Ann Louise Gilligan have reclaimed the word 'wife'. When Ms Gilligan died in 2017, many indeed were the tributes to the ideal wife who had brought such conjugal contentment to her wife.

Not all gay feminists endorse same-sex marriage. It is rejected by the feminist lawyer Julie Bindel as a mere copycat model of heterosexual marriage. For similar reasons, the influential Judith Butler rejects it as symbolising a 'norm'. It can be an option, but it shouldn't be an ideal.

Still, the notion of equal marriage has put marriage itself into a new and much more positive light, which is one of those fascinating quirks of social history.

Media

I've earned my living in the media for over five decades, and over that span much has changed in terms of values, attitudes, political ideas, sexism, feminism and technology. In general, the media tends to reflect, fairly accurately, the values of its time. *The Times* of London published a lot of cartoons about the Irish looking like baboons in the Victorian era because a lot of people thought that was funny. And a lot of people were irritated by the Irish as they were poor, complaining, rebellious Roman Catholics, or a people trying to assassinate Queen Victoria (seven attempts, although not exclusively from Irishmen).

The media often made fun of feminism in the past, but as more and more feminist goals were successfully achieved, it came to support it, and then to claim it.

The media always reflects the value of the time. Dissidents against the *zeitgeist* will become marginalised voices.

Men excluding women

Professor Mary Beard, the distinguished academic of the ancient world, has written that men deliberately exclude women from positions of power. This is sometimes true: although men also exclude other men from power on grounds of class, status, religion and tribe. Men kill other men a lot more than they kill women as a way of eliminating rivals. In that sense, the female of the species is a lot less deadly than the male.

But the theme of men excluding women from the corridors of power is illuminated in story and fable by Rudyard Kipling's poem, 'The Female of the Species', first published in 1919. It describes the way in which men fear women, fear that the power given to her by the maternal instinct can make her ferocious and even toxic: 'She who faces Death by torture for each life beneath her breast/ May not deal with doubt or pity, must not swerve for fact or jest.' Kipling's view is, of course, reductive: women are not defined by the maternal instinct, though we see that it can be fierce across all species. And women did face 'death by torture' in pregnancy and childbirth, over countless centuries, for the sake of motherhood – it's no joke. But it's not true that women do not deal with doubt or pity: evolutionary psychologists say that females often have more empathy, and the psychologist Carol Gilligan has found that women are often more capable of understanding nuance, ambiguity and contradictions than men.

Kipling sees man excluding woman as an essential cowardliness of male bonding, and male jokiness ('mirth obscene'). 'So it comes that man, the coward, when he gathers to confer/ With his fellow-braves in council, dare not leave a place for her.' Is this why so many males, for so long, chose to keep females out of golf clubs, other clubs and from around the conference table? Kipling discloses his own fellow-feeling with 'man a bear in most relations – worm and savage otherwise' and his fear of the lash of a woman's tongue: 'Speech that drips, corrodes and poisons'.

The Female of the Species

When the Himalayan peasant meets the he-bear in his pride,
He shouts to scare the monster, who will often turn aside.
But the she-bear thus accosted rends the peasant tooth
and nail.
For the female of the species is more deadly than the male.

When Nag the basking cobra hears the careless foot of man,
He will sometimes wriggle sideways and avoid it if he can.
But his mate makes no such motion where she camps beside
the trail.
For the female of the species is more deadly than the male.

When the early Jesuit fathers preached to Hurons and Choctaws,
They prayed to be delivered from the vengeance of the squaws.
'Twas the women, not the warriors, turned those stark
enthusiasts pale.
For the female of the species is more deadly than the male.

Man's timid heart is bursting with the things he must not say,
For the Woman that God gave him isn't his to give away;
But when hunter meets with husband, each confirms the
    other's tale –
The female of the species is more deadly than the male.

Man, a bear in most relations, worm and savage otherwise,
Man propounds negotiations, Man accepts the compromise.
Very rarely will he squarely push the logic of a fact
To its ultimate conclusion in unmitigated act.

Fear, or foolishness, impels him, ere he lay the wicked low,
To concede some form of trial even to his fiercest foe.
Mirth obscene diverts his anger – Doubt and Pity oft perplex
Him in dealing with an issue – to the scandal of The Sex!

But the Woman that God gave him, every fibre of her frame
Proves her launched for one sole issue, armed and engined
    for the same;
And to serve that single issue, lest the generations fail,
The female of the species must be deadlier than the male.

She who faces Death by torture for each life beneath her breast
May not deal in doubt or pity – must not swerve for fact or jest.
These be purely male diversions – not in these her honour
    dwells –
She the Other Law we live by, is that Law and nothing else.
She can bring no more to living than the powers that make
    her great
As the Mother of the Infant and the Mistress of the Mate.

And when Babe and Man are lacking and she strides
    unclaimed to claim

Her right as femme (and baron), her equipment is the same.
She is wedded to convictions – in default of grosser ties;
Her contentions are her children, Heaven help him who denies!–

He will meet no suave discussion, but the instant, white-hot, wild,
Wakened female of the species warring as for spouse and child.
Unprovoked and awful charges – even so the she-bear fights,
Speech that drips, corrodes, and poisons – even so the cobra bites,

Scientific vivisection of one nerve till it is raw
And the victim writhes in anguish – like the Jesuit with the squaw!
So it comes that Man, the coward, when he gathers to confer
With his fellow-braves in council, dare not leave a place for her

Where, at war with Life and Conscience, he uplifts his err-ing hands
To some God of Abstract Justice – which no woman under-stands.
And Man knows it! Knows, moreover, that the Woman that God gave him
Must command but may not govern – shall enthral but not enslave him.
And *She* knows, because *She* warns him, and Her instincts never fail,
That the Female of Her Species is more deadly than the Male.

Menopause

There are reasons why some women prefer not to be public about their experience of the menopause. If a woman is moody, volatile, irritable, irrational, depressed (even suicidal), sleepless and prone to hot flushes, she may consider that this condition, if known about, disadvantages her in the workplace. A feminist who affirms her ability to be equal may not wish to be called 'menopausal', this having sometimes been a code-word for 'bonkers'. An American vice-president, Hubert Humphreys, said it could be very dangerous to have a 'menopausal woman's' finger on the nuclear button – or, indeed, have an irrational, menopausal woman in charge of any responsible decisions. (He was speaking during an election campaign, a time when politicians are apt to utter a great deal of adversarial verbiage to deter competitors.)

Simone de Beauvoir herself was not very complimentary about menopausal women. One should be wary of women between the ages of fifty and fifty-five, she wrote:

'Instead of fighting off despair, she often chooses to yield to its intoxication. She harps endlessly on her wrongs, her regrets, her reproaches; she imagines her relatives and neighbours guilty of dark machinations against her; if there is a sister or a friend of her own age closely associated with her life, they may together

build up delusions of persecution... Cases of patho-
logical jealousy are most numerous between the ages
of fifty and fifty-five.'

With such attitudes against woman in their fifties, it's understandable that some have wished to brush the matter aside,
feeling that it is no help to feminism. Anyway, some women
sail through it without being much troubled.

But some women really do endure such a dreadful ordeal
at that passage of life once known as 'the change' that they
need to talk about it: to get the proper medical help, and
even, perhaps, to help others articulate their experiences.

Carol Vorderman, well-liked as a television presenter (and
a brilliant mathematician), has felt the need to talk publicly
about what afflictions she endured while experiencing the
menopause. She would wake up feeling that life had 'no
point' anymore: she'd 'start sobbing' and 'felt wretched for
no reason. It wasn't as if I was grieving or anything had gone
wrong. Far from it; I'm fortunate – there was just no joy in
anything.' She could feel suicidal. 'It was so wretched; so,
so horrible. It's difficult to explain, but the world seemed
dark and you could be in a lovely place and feel nothing,
no pleasure at all.' She was exhausted and barely slept. She
is a divorcee with two adult children, and had an ailing
mother who she helped to care for, as well as a working life
to maintain. In one sense, these responsibilities helped her
to get through each day; however awful she felt, she told
herself, 'Carol, you have children. Stop, stop, stop!'

She sought help with an expert on menopausal depression
(Professor John Studd), and he prescribed the right cocktail
of bio-identical hormones (based on natural plants), and
eventually, aged fifty-four, she came through. It's possible

that she might have come through anyway, but when you need medical help, it's right to get it. She also received thousands of messages from other women with similar symptoms who felt supported by her open attitude.

If some women would prefer to keep the issue of the menopause private (as would some men), it's likely that many women suffered too much in silence over the taboo of not speaking about it. The pioneering Victorian feminist and educationalist Dorothea Beale experienced what was evidently a profound menopausal depression, which included a despairing loss of faith, a very serious case for a woman to whom spiritual faith had been previously very important. Referring to this wretched period in Dorothea's life, her biographer Josephine Kamm writes:

'There is no record of the precise nature of Dorothea's illness, but as the birthday was her forty-seventh it is not very difficult to guess. Even with the medical alleviations in use today there is scarcely a woman who can weather this difficult period of her life in complete physical and mental serenity; and in the last century mental disturbance, either temporary or permanent, was not at all uncommon. Such an indelicate subject could not be discussed; and if Dorothea mentioned it to her doctors or to one or two intimate friends, no one seems to have suggested that her physical symptoms and her spiritual anguish were most closely interrelated.'

Yet, having passed the age of disparaging Victorian coyness, Josephine Kamm – writing in 1954 – cannot bring herself to do anything further than allude to 'this difficult period', rather than use the proper word – menopause.

In the service of the correct description of a human condition, it is good to have liberated the word 'menopause' from its cloaked position, but with the additional coda that some women want to be frank about it, while some women do not, either from privacy, from concerns about being considered irrational, or from the subjective position that it simply didn't bother them one bit.

Germaine Greer sees the menopause as something to be proud of. It's a privilege to grow older, to grow wiser, even to become a crone.

There's an anthropological insight on menopause which I find fascinating – it appears in Sheila Kitzinger's book, *Women as Mothers*. Mrs Kitzinger suggests that women in some Asian cultures such as India or Japan, tend to experience the menopause less distressingly, because of the respect and honour that is traditionally accorded to the older matriarch in these societies. Individual cases will surely differ across any society, but if the body and the mind are interconnected in mood, then it is possible that in western cultures we may regard the perceived loss of sex appeal – and fertility choice – in mid-life as a contributory factor to mid-life crises, in contrast to the perceived enhancement of status that age may bring in others.

Menstruation

In the film *20th Century Women*, a young woman, Abbey (played by Greta Gerwig), demands that a group assembled around a supper party say the word 'menstruation', explaining that she is at present menstruating. She urges the folk who identify themselves as laid-back, even Bohemian Californians, to say the word *menstruation, menstruation.* Somewhat hesitantly, some do. But Annette Bening's character, Dorothea, though a liberated woman of her time – 1979 – and a single mother by choice and against conventional wisdom, finds this objectionable, particularly as it involves her fifteen-year-old son obediently reciting 'menstruation'. She breaks up the soiree and afterwards tasks Abbey with pushing 'hardcore feminism' at a teenage boy trying to find his way.

How would any of us respond if we'd been sitting around that table with Abbey urging us to repeat 'menstruation, menstruation'? I'd have welcomed an interesting argument. I'd have put it to Abbey that menstruation was, in ancient matriarchal societies, a symbol of women's power, of her connection with the moon's cycles, and thus, too, of woman's capacity to wax and wane in mood.

In the same way that Indian women wear henna, it is an echo of this old, matriarchal power. It has sometimes occurred to me that red nail polish might be an unconscious allusion to the menstrual blood of matriarchal power.

124

When sanitary towels are advertised on TV, the public does not like to see red painted fingernails in the same frame, I'm told. As the market usually follows public taste, red-tipped fingernails and sanitary towels will never be shown together.

But the power of menstrual blood is also a secret power. It is all part of women's secrets that are withheld from men. I wonder if making a mixed group chant 'menstruation' is actually giving away woman's power?

Dorothea has grown up in a world which would have regarded periods, certainly, as something private – and sometimes, privacy can be associated with both silence and shame. American culture of the twentieth century was particularly keen on hygiene, and many may have shared an 'unclean' view of menstruation. Doris Lessing, feminist icon, has written about her sense of distaste for menstruation. 'I like the smell of sex, of sweat, of skin or hair. But the faintly dubious, essentially stale smell of menstrual blood, I hate. And resent. It is a … bad smell, emanating from me.'

Lessing would very probably have had the same reaction as Dorothea in *20th Century Women*.

But, as in all subjects that are explored in their complexity, there are paradoxes. Women in western culture have generally taken the idea that periods should be treated with discretion. Semitic culture – both Jewish and Islamic – has been much more open about the issue. Muslim women are excused from all household chores while they are menstruating, and a late friend of mine had a vivid lesson in this.

One day she was shopping in Kensington while she was experiencing a particularly heavy period. She lived with her husband and two children in a top-storey flat which had no lift, so she was accustomed to heaving the bags of shopping up four floors. Standing in line at the supermarket, she found herself behind a Muslim man who was also doing the family shopping. The Muslim man's shopping trolley contained the usual array of goods, including a supply of sanitary towels and tampons.

As my friend stood there, she thought: 'This man's wife is in purdah because she's menstruating – probably lying back on a sofa reading a good book – so he has to do all the shopping and skivvying. I'm menstruating and have to keep on with my normal chores. Which of us, I wonder, would call ourselves the more liberated?'

Money thoughts

I once gave a women's lunch party in my Dublin flat; most of the attendees had been involved in the feminist movement and were now approaching middle age. The question posed was: 'What has been the greatest benefit to women in our lifetimes?'

Answers there were many. 'The contraceptive pill.' 'The motor car.' 'The washing machine, the deep freeze, the microwave.' 'The end of corsets.' 'Jeans.' 'Divorce.' 'Elective caesarians.' But my late friend, the novelist Clare Boylan, came up with this answer: 'Money.' The ability to earn money, bank it, own it, control it, invest it and do whatever the heck you wanted with it – was the greatest benefit to women.

This is a true insight, though it's possibly not entirely new. There was a time when dowries were considered of benefit to women, since it gave them power and choice (more in some systems than it others.) In John B. Keane's immortal play *Big Maggie*, the domineering matriarch underlines her power with the words: 'I brought a fortune into this farm!' Many a matriarch felt empowered by that financial cushion behind them and gained respect through the wider extended kin because she had 'means'.

I have earned my own living throughout my working life (which began at the age of sixteen), but I've never felt either confident or liberated about handling money. For a reason I cannot fully understand or explain, money is mixed up with feelings of guilt (that is, unworthiness), and at the same time, resentment (if I've worked so hard, and earned so much over the course of my life, why am I not rich?). In some ways, it's a more complicated subject than sex.

Is this for reasons of gender, or for reasons of culture and heritability? My parents were bourgeois-bohemians who thought it 'vulgar' to discuss money. They would have been wholly with Yeats and his attitudes to 'the greasy till' of small shopkeepers who 'add the ha'pence to the pence'. They too had 'means' in their time, but never seemed to have any later on.

Christianity also has tradition of despising money ('Consider the lilies of the fields...') and sometimes, when you see what is done for gain – murder, the swindling of old-age pensioners, cheating and lying – you think St Paul must have had a point: 'The love of money is the root of all evil.' This must have been influential. But is money a feminist issue? Decidedly so.

Motherhood

(1)

When I first became a mother, my friend and colleague Maureen Cleave said to me: 'For the rest of your life, until you go down into the grave yourself, your thoughts will be on the child, or children, you have brought into the world. Your thoughts, your concerns, your worries will focus daily on them, and displace many of the concerns and ambitions you have for yourself.'

Motherhood is a very big subject, and central to feminism, since it usually sets up stresses and tensions for any ambitious woman. But what Maureen said to me on this subject has remained engraved on my heart.

(2) Motherhood's intensification

Birth control has made motherhood a choice, in that young women can and do think about whether they wish to be mothers in a way that wasn't routine in the past. (The irrepressible Princess Anne once called motherhood 'a professional hazard of being a wife', and that's exactly how it was seen.) It is good that motherhood should be voluntary. But something that is voluntary carries more responsibility than something that just happens, in the general course of nature.

Marriage now does not necessarily include the motherhood package. Feminists often write articles about their

129

entitlement to be mated, but child-free. But motherhood, if more voluntary, has also been intensified.

Fewer children means more of a focus on each child – it is evident that you can give more attention to two children than to twelve. Commercial pressures: it hasn't escaped the notice of Mothercare and other retailers selling to the mums' market that parents and grandparents buy a lot of things for their offspring, and, therefore, there are even more products to sell to them. Higher standards of living and education put more pressure on parents to attain and achieve more. Child-centered education has added to parental pressure: once the teachers and schools were just expected to get on with the job – now parents are involved at all points. The deplorable phenomenon of the Chinese 'Tiger Mothers' who urge their children on to even greater achievements has raised the bar, yet again, for mothers. These are accompanied, sometimes, by 'helicopter parents' who hover over their children's every move.

Children are – rightly – seen as very, very precious. As a result, they are much more protected. I walked to school from the age of five. This would be considered a serious case of child neglect today. (There were, it must be said, fewer cars in the 1950s, and they went at a much slower pace.)
  Gender theory is playing its own part in the 'intensification' of motherhood. If everything is a social construct, then every woman is responsible for the kind of mother she becomes, and the quality of parenting she dishes out. From serial killers to dysfunctional comics, much is blamed on bad mothering. When hapless outcomes were blamed on 'the will of God' or 'Kismet', motherhood was in some respects an easier gig. Or at any rate, a more forgiving one.

Nature

Everything 'natural' is now extolled (if preceded by 'organic', even more so), but 'nature' is a tricky concept in the feminist canon. There's a certain anxiety that it means sending women back to the kitchen sink, pregnant and barefoot. 'Natural' distinctions between the sexes are regarded with suspicion, lest they prove reactionary. Differences are often analysed as being socially constructed (see Gender Theory).

We can see civilization as an endless struggle against nature (gardening, dentistry, corrective glasses), or, hippy-like, white-witch-pagan worship of it. With measured approach we can seek a middle ground, though extremes often drive the argument. The Victorians disliked Darwinism not just because it challenged the Bible, but because (as they saw it) it seemed to place us nearer to the monkeys than the angels. A similar view can still be taken of Nature v. Socialisation. We can take sides, seek the balance, or consider that the jury is still out.

Nomenclature

When the American feminist Sheila Michaels died in 2017, aged seventy-eight, she was admired for launching the honorific 'Ms', intended to replace both 'Miss' and 'Mrs' as a way of addressing and describing women, without reference to their married or unmarried status. Sheila Michaels didn't invent it – it first appeared in 1901 – but when she glimpsed it on a label, she saw the opportunity to use it, and embarked on a campaign to have it accepted. When Gloria Steinem took it up for the title of her feminist magazine, 'Ms' was well and truly launched, and has now been established in the lexicon – more or less excluding the previous 'Miss', now only used in an ironic way (although long used, with honour, in the performing arts: Elizabeth Taylor, seven times married, was still addressed, respectfully, as 'Miss Taylor').

Sheila Michaels' own quest for a more neutral moniker was also a quest for a kind of privacy. At the age of twenty-two, she disliked employers asking her if she was a Miss or a Mrs. What business was it of theirs? Good point. There was a family context too: she was the daughter of her mother's secret lover, and brought up by her grandparents. There was ambiguity about her surname, and a sense that her father had spurned her. 'I didn't belong to my father and I didn't belong to a husband. I hadn't seen very many marriages I wanted to emulate.' So 'Ms' had an ideological context as well as being a convenient form of address.

My late brother was a bank manager, and though he was conservative on social matters, he welcomed the use of 'Ms' because he felt it was more tactful for single mothers. There was a time when it was a matter of shame to give birth while still retaining the title of Miss. There were even punitive midwives who would do a deliberately demeaning roll-call in a labour ward: 'Mrs Brown, Mrs Carter, Mrs Davis, MISS Finnegan, Mrs Grey, Mrs Harris...'

So 'Ms' took off in the 1970s and 1980s, and very useful it became too. It prompted many discussions about how the system of nomenclature should be changed for women. Why should a woman take a man's name in marriage? Actually, it was never a legal requirement, but it was the usual practice. Why not follow the Icelandic idea and name men after their fathers ('Johannson') and women after their mothers ('Ingridsdottir')? Except that the population of Iceland is hardly greater than the city of Cork, and in small populations, names can be simplified because everyone knows who everyone is anyway – in Wales, the many people with the surnames of 'Jones' were also easily identified by vocation ('Jones the Postman').

A woman can keep her own name, but even her own name is a patronymic – that is, it's her father's name (my father having been Patrick Kenny). It's a free choice, but if there are children, it doesn't always seem a practical one. If a family of four are traveling together – particularly in these days of tight airport security and suspicion falling on anything unusual – it is sensible for all to have the same surname. Of course it can be the woman's name as much as the man's, if all are agreed.

I added 'West' to my legal name after marriage and children, just as Hillary Clinton called herself, for many years, Hillary Rodham Clinton; but I can't say it is without complications. My credit card says 'Mary Kenny', while my passport says 'Mary Kenny West', and there was trouble, on one particular occasion, when due to board a plane to Australia, because the names did not coordinate. More recently, the British driving licence authority, the DVLA, withheld a renewed driving licence from me, having accused me of changing my identity – because a hyphen had appeared in my name on some documents, rendering Kenny West as Kenny-West. They wanted to confiscate my passport as a verification process: it took six weeks of to-ing and fro-ing of much documentation before it was sorted and I eventually managed to convince them that I was not an imposter. This is a small illustration of some the issues that may lurk around the question of nomenclature, which is a more complex subject than it seems.

'Ms' remains handy because it can cover a multitude. Women who have been divorced may still bear the name of a former husband and retain it for professional reasons. Angela Merkel continues to bear the name of a former husband, mainly, I would suppose, for 'brand' reasons – that is how she is recognised. Yet, out of respect for her seniority, she is often described as 'Mrs' (*Frau*).

The style rules around female nomenclature are highly inconsistent. Theresa May (née Brazier) has made it clear that she wishes to be known by her married name and if given an honorific, is called 'Mrs May'. But not by everyone: the *Irish Times* has a house style which insists on referring to her as 'Ms May' – not because the lady herself has chosen it, but because the editor of the newspaper thinks this is fitting.

Yet the former President of Ireland, Mary Robinson, who also chose to use her married name (though I personally thought that her patronymic was more distinguished – Bourke, being an old Anglo-Norman clan intermarried with Granuaile, the pirate queen of Connaught), is often referred to as 'Mrs Robinson', rather than 'Ms'.

Nicola Sturgeon prefers 'Ms' – it's not her married name anyway, so that's logical. Arlene Foster uses 'Mrs' (her own family name was Kelly), but depending on the mood and attitude of the style arbiter, she may be Ms or Mrs.

Sometimes a woman absolutely affirms that she wishes to be a Mrs. Amal Alamuddin, distinguished human rights lawyer, signaled that she wished to be known as Mrs George Clooney. Context is interesting: this was interpreted not as a signal of deference by the beautiful and accomplished Amal, but as a sign of her confidence in her own identity and her gracious choice to bestow upon her husband the honour of using his name.

Sometimes a woman will use both: Cherie Blair, married to former prime minister Tony Blair, is Mrs Blair on the occasions when she accompanies him, but Cherie Booth in her working life as a lawyer.

Sometimes there are sensible reasons to choose one or the other. Hillary Clinton dropped the 'Rodham' from her portmanteau name – because Clinton was the better-established brand. A politician needs profile and recognition more than she needs to make a point about her patronymic.

And some style arbiters drop all honorifics. When Sheila Michaels died, the *Guardian* did not call her 'Ms Michaels': they just called her 'Michaels'. Personally, I loathe being called 'Kenny', because there are so many people with the same surname; it leads to confusion, and can be short for

'Kenneth' as a first name. But usually, I just don't get to choose. It's the style arbiter that chooses what a woman gets to be called.

Using only the surname reduces the clarity of context. I read a report which made reference to the public careers of Hillary Clinton, Bill Clinton and their daughter Chelsea Clinton. It was 'Clinton this' and 'Clinton that', and it was difficult to figure out who was doing what when. With the proliferation of dynasties this often occurs: a young actor (self-defined) Zoe Kazan, whose father and grandfather (the great Elia Kazan) are associated with the film business, is described at interview as 'Kazan', and you're not terribly sure which family member is being referred to.

The etiquette rule should be (in my view) that individuals are entitled to be called whatever they wish to be called. 'Ms' was a useful and enlightened addition to the range of choices (and we now have the gender-neutral 'Mx' as well). A range of choices for men have been introduced by HSBC bank. But the more choice, the more complications. And the more complications, the more likely a hierarchy will develop. To some extent it has already happened, when 'Ms' is perceived as the junior version of 'Mrs'.

Omitted from the record:
invisible women

The presence of women is often either absent or invisible in the public square of history. This can be seen by the measurement of any collection of obituaries throughout the twentieth century. *The Times*'s compendium of 'Great Lives', for example, republished 123 obituaries from that London newspaper from 1916 to 2005, of whom just twenty-four are women, and some women chosen appeared on account of their rank and position as wives and mothers (Queen Elizabeth; the Queen Mother; Diana, Princess of Wales; Jacqueline Kennedy Onassis; Raisa Gorbachev) rather than for any outstanding independent achievement, while those absent include Rosa Luxembourg, Simone de Beauvoir, Hannah Arendt, Rosalind Franklin, Barbara Moore, Dorothy Parker, Flannery O'Connor, Dolores Ibarruri, Marie Stopes, Edith Stein, the tennis ace Suzanne Lenglen, the dancer Anna Pavlova, the inspiring military painter Lady Butler and many more do not appear.

The Times' compilation of Great Irish Lives, edited by Charles Lysaght, is even more revealing of a pattern of invisibility in *Times* obituaries: women don't really appear in significant numbers until around the 1990s. And where their lives were noted, they were remarkably sketchy. The editors and their selections reflect broadly how things were as fewer women did emerge in the public realm. Perhaps it's gratifying to note that the balance of obituaries of the distinguished is now being corrected, and the main newspapers are now much more inclined to observe the passing of women of achievement. Obituary editors are also more aware of correcting the imbalance, and that is surely thanks to feminism.

Traditionally, men were seen to be more visible in the public realm, as any picture or photograph of a meaningful gathering will usually reveal: the historic picture, say, of the signing of the Treaty of Rome in 1956, the founding occasion of the European Union, is 100 per cent masculine. Women were accorded influence and sometimes power in the private sphere. A visit to a graveyard will reveal how many tombs pay tribute to dearly loved mothers, wives, sisters, daughters. They were not invisible to those who loved them.

But it's perhaps also true to say that in dedicating themselves to their families, many women in the past were unable to fulfill their talents and pursue their aspirations. We've tried to correct that, too, in our time.

Ordeals remembered:
the dance floor

There was a ghastly ritual expected of young women when I was a teenager. You were enjoined to attend 'hops' (and later on, as an adult, an even more arcane rite very popular in Ireland known as 'the dress dance'). 'Hops' were local dances, often associated with a tennis association or a rugby club. Fortunately I was unable to attend the tennis 'hop' because the local one was run by a Protestant sports club, and they didn't admit Catholics (for fear of a 'mixed' marriage ensuing). But towards a rugby 'hop' I was directed, aged fifteen. This involved groups of girls clustering together – sometimes in the ladies' loos, repairing or enhancing their cosmetic presentation and chattering away inanely – or else lining up against the walls, waiting – *waiting!* – for the guys to arrive, and invite them to dance.

The guys were in the pub, where they tanked up, presumably to work up the nerve to ask some female to take the floor, the invitation usually being a jerk of the head and then an unsteady steering around the ballroom. I wanted to take the initiative in anything I chose to do, and instead of attending Saturday night hops, I took to attending the theatre instead. I never did get the point of 'dress dances', which occurred when men and women were in their twenties and thirties (and usually took place in January and February, being in the run-up to Lent, and thus a kind of Irish version of Mardi Gras). They now compose a social archive in such publications as *Irish Tatler & Sketch* (and make an interesting contrast to the collective misery-memoir of Irish social history): nice middle-class girls in glamorous strapless evening frocks, with the escorts who often became their grooms.

But reaction against the passive role of waiting to be asked turned me on a different path, towards independence, self-affirmation and being my own person.

The dance, in other contexts, can be an agency of liberation: the joy of movement, of bodily expression, of the 'evocation poetique' of the ballet and modern dance. And disco-dancing is another world away – fluid, even gender-neutral. But for me, the teenage dance ritual made me understand that I never wanted to have to wait to be chosen by anyone.

Patriarchy

'The patriarchy' and 'patriarchal attitudes' are the recognised culprits of women's oppression through the centuries; and it is for sure that public institutions have been constructed by (and mostly for) men. Regard any historic photograph of an esteemed institution (the House of Commons, the House of Representatives, the United Nations, the European Community, the City of London, the Royal Society of Architects, the Royal Academy of Engineers, the Nobel Prize Committee, the leadership of the Trade Unions, the fellows of Oxford University, the Praesidium of the Soviet Union, the composition of the Académie Française, the ruling elite of the Gaelic Athletic Association – need I go on?) and, until recent times, these were, without exception, heavily, often exclusively masculine in composition. So men ruled the world, or at least, the public world: and that's what 'patriarchy' means, kind of – rule by the father.

And yet, getting down to 'the personal is political', the incidence of actual 'patriarchs' I have known over the course of my lifetime is surprisingly few, and decisively outnumbered by males of a very different ilk: I've known men who were hopeless, feckless, penniless, faithless and useless, abandoning fathers, bigamist husbands, cadgers, bounders, blubbers, soaks, hen-pecked weaklings, maladroit adulterers, two-timing love-rats, narcissistic popinjays, unreliable gigolos, chancers, bores, boasters, swindlers, fraudsters, tightwads (the rich guys who let you pick up the taxi fare), gamblers, work-shy idlers, egocentric hedonists, spoiled brats, needy wheedlers, oddbods, poltroons, creeps, recluses, neurotics, hypochondriacs, cry-babies, commitment-phobes, voyeurs, Andy Caps who never get up, Peter Pans who never grow up, upper-class twits, lower-class plonkers, fantasists, fatuous dunces, spendthrifts, embezzlers, sex slaves to dominatrix houris, incorrigible *habitués* of the betting shop and the race track, and guys who run off with all their wife's credit cards (and a nineteen-year-old blonde).

When I review the repertory of my experience – I suppose that's what comes of hanging around Fleet Street and Soho – I wonder where all the 'patriarchs' are. Have I ever actually known a patriarch, leaving aside the odd alpha-male newspaper editor (Rommels in the office, pussycat at home)? But I've known women who went out charring to support a hopeless man, women traipsing devotedly on prison visits to bring comfort to their bloke who has never done an honest day's work – and never will – sisters and wives attending therapy meetings trying to save a brother or a husband from killing himself with alcohol or opiates, shattered womenfolk at funerals for the suicide of their precious boy, ageing prostitutes still on the game to provide for a heedless lover who must have the latest bling for his dude-about-town self-presentation.

I used to listen to my aunts talking when I was young. Their overweening fear was that a young lad would turn out to be a 'ne'er do well'. In other words, they seemed more worried that a male would not take on the responsible cloak of patriarchy, than that he would. I report this as a witness to history, quite neutrally.

Political Women

It is great to see so many women gaining prominence and success in politics. There was a photograph taken of Theresa May, Angela Merkel and the Polish prime minister Beata Szydo in a meeting, and it was just a normal meeting between three political leaders. Nobody said – 'look, woman leaders!'

In the United Kingdom in 2017, there are three national women leaders: Theresa May in Westminster, Nicola Sturgeon in Scotland and Arlene Foster in Northern Ireland. In Scotland itself, all three principle party leaders are women.

Women are making terrific progress in politics, and feminists are campaigning for even more political participation. Some eventually hope to see all parliaments fifty-fifty. But to be honest, 'more women' usually means 'more women of the kind we like'. Marine Le Pen in France – who leads the National Front, as well as quite a significant movement, and was elected to the National Assembly – attracted not a single nod of approval from any feminist movement.

The day after Emmanuel Macron's victory, *Woman's Hour* on BBC Radio 4 extolled Brigitte Macron as the most wonderful role model for women, while disparaging Marine Le Pen. People are free to choose whatever role models they like, but it is worth mentioning that Marine Le Pen did lead a political party through the democratic process of standing for election, however much one dislikes the policies, and did get duly elected to the National Assembly, whereas Brigitte Macron's achievement is being an attractive and successful wife. She is certainly a clever, inspirational person in her own right, but political achievement does involve the vote.

Post-feminism and Paglia

Post-feminism is defined as a critical way of thinking about feminism; the celebrity post-feminist is, surely, Camille Paglia, an eccentric but dazzlingly brilliant Italian-American academic. I've seen her in action – in interview with Claire Fox – and it's pretty challenging to keep up with her machine-gun-fire conversation, in which knowledge and ideas tumble out with stunning fluency amid encyclopaedic references to history, language, literature and the classical world. She's a gay woman and often full of contradictions.

She's an atheist who nonetheless reveres religion as a source of culture, refinement, and a human need. She's pro-abortion (she eschews the word 'pro-choice' as 'a cowardly euphemism') and has contributed to Planned Parenthood since her youth, and supports, unreservedly, women's access to abortion services. And yet she writes: 'I profoundly respect the pro-life viewpoint, which I think has the moral high ground. The violence intrinsic to abortion cannot be wished away by magical thinking. Abortion pits the stronger against the weaker, and only one survives.'

As a lesbian, she loves women – she has worshipped Katherine Hepburn, Ava Gardner, Madonna – but she also admires men for what they have achieved, even under the greatest disadvantages. 'Homer and Milton were blind: can we claim that being female is a worse handicap than being blind?' She urges us to look admiringly, not grudgingly, at what men have wrought in so many fields of endeavor, and under Paglia's influence, I have looked with awe at great engineering feats accomplished by men, from suspension bridges to the amazing and extraordinary Channel Tunnel, which zooms us from London (and Ashford) to Paris (and Brussels, and soon further afield).

She sees women occupying a virtuous middle of the human spectrum rather than the extremes of good or bad. 'There is no female Mozart because there is no female Jack the Ripper.'

Paglia thinks civilisation has progressed by thwarting and frustrating nature – homosexuality is social advancement precisely because it is frustrating nature's promptings towards Darwinist reproduction. But the power of nature is always hovering, and can overwhelm us at any moment. 'Let nature shrug, and all is in ruin. Fire, flood, lightning, tornado, hurricane, volcano, earthquake – anywhere at any time.' And she sees sex as part of nature – it has to be tamed, but it is there. 'Sexual freedom, sexual liberation. A modern delusion. Sex is a far darker power than feminism has admitted. Behaviourist sex therapies believe guiltless, no-fault sex is possible. But sex has always been girt around with taboo, irrespective of culture... Sex is daemonic. The search for freedom through sex is doomed to failure. In sex, compulsion and ancient necessity rule.'

Paglia is a courageous, sometimes reckless, original thinker. Her values are both modern and ancient: she affirms all the freedoms of a contemporary, highly educated, extraordinarily confident American woman. She is supremely independent. She owes nothing to anyone, and nothing holds her back. She is not afraid to offend, as, if truth be told, most of us probably are. But – and perhaps some of her apparent contradictions arise here – she is also profoundly attached to her Italian family and heritage, which included a strong kinship network of matriarchs – and nuns, and through Catholic imagery, a cultural link to the ancient world of mother-worship and pagan-infused sexual drama.

Pornography

I arrived late for the Cambridge Union debate at which I was due to speak – I often arrived late for events at a time in my life when I was juggling childcare, work and extra-mural activities like university debates. The moral purity campaigner Mary Whitehouse was already on her feet, inveighing against the corruption and general wickedness of pornography, which was spreading its disgusting tentacles through the media and society. What was striking was the battery of boiler-suited militant feminists punching the air with clenched fists, shouting in evident solidarity, 'Right on, Mary!'

An epiphany moment in the 1980s. Radical feminists were backing Mary Whitehouse in her moral crusade against porn. Mind you, it had happened before. Many of the Suffragettes were crusaders for moral purity – Christabel Pankhurst's slogan was: 'Votes for Women – And Chastity for Men!' Damer Dawson, a celebrated feminist of the early part of the twentieth century (and motor-racing ace) became one of the most enthusiastic supporters of the Irish censorship regulations, which sought to exclude 'the tide of filth' allegedly infecting literature after the 1920s.

Many influential feminists of our time, such as Catharine MacKinnon and Andrea Dworkin, have seen pornography as one of the greatest evils, contributing to the 'objectification' of women, and prompting a 'culture of rape'. Pornography proceeds from misogyny, in this school of thought – and begets more misogyny, too.

I daresay it does. It's rather unsettling that there seems to be so much of it about, and that what was once available through selected publications is now easily accessible through the internet. But there's a problem here: if you believe in free speech and free expression, you have to accept that there will be bad stuff available as well as admirable stuff. And it's hard to escape the widespread evidence that men like to look at sexy pictures of women more than women like to look at sexy pictures of men. I'm sure there is a market for female erotica, but I can't think of many multi-millionaires who have built their fortunes on this basis, so it can't be very copious.

The porn business tends to show that men and women are different, and behave differently. Porn is bought by men; romance is bought by women. Generalisations, true, but broadly exact. Ask the editors at Mills & Boon.

Incidentally, although I admired Mrs Whitehouse's guts, commitment and sheer nerve in standing up to an establishment that was condescending towards her (the BBC were Oxbridge men: she was just a common little Birmingham housewife), I was on the opposite side of the Cambridge debate. Even when what it produces is hateful, there must be liberty.

Power

Power is said to define relationships: racism can only be by a white person against a person of colour because the white person is considered to have the power. Because male power has been exercised over females, the exploitation of power is usually thought to be from male to female.

I find it a more mysterious element. I have watched power-politics within offices, and it's interesting how some individuals – not necessarily defined by gender – are very clever at manipulating office politics, and some are completely without such skills. I would rather have influence than power, so perhaps I haven't paid sufficient attention to its wielding.

Pregnancy perceived

It's rather cheering to see pregnancy flaunted – as in the craze for posing in the nude and showing off 'the bump'. This was first done, sensationally, by Demi Moore for *Vanity Fair* in 1997, at a time when the middle-aged could recall women's magazines being full of advice about how to tactfully conceal an expectant condition. Look up those pictures of Jacqueline Kennedy in 1960, when her husband was first elected to the White House: Mrs Kennedy's clothes and careful way of sitting were discreetly arranged so that the eye was not drawn to 'the bump'. Expectant mothers were advised to wear something white near to the face, as a distraction from the swelling fruitfulness of the body. Pregnancy was once termed as 'being confined'.

We now live in a more candid age. A more active, and a more confident age. Pregnancy was sometimes concealed, or discreetly robed because of the uncertainty of outcome. There could be a miscarriage. The baby could die. The mother could die. These were, as Kipling writes in 'The Female of Species', serious matters. Maternity made women fierce – life was not a joke – because so much was at stake: 'She who faces Death by torture for each life beneath her breast/May not deal in doubt or pity – must not swerve for fact or jest.'

But as the dangers of pregnancy recede – thankfully – so confidence grows. Proudly flaunting the pregnant body – as done by Beyoncé and Serena Williams – is an expression of that female confidence. Tennis-players are, these days, glorifying in pregnancy. When the Luxembourg player Maria Minella, a tennis ace, lost to her Italian opponent at Wimbledon, she announced that she was four and a half months pregnant, and subsequently received an avalanche of congratulations, She said it was wonderful to get such a reaction – and she'd be back at Wimbledon with the baby. Progress has wrought a welcoming attitude to motherhood in sport.

Pregnancy experienced

Simone de Beauvoir saw pregnancy, critically, as 'the bondage of reproduction', and 'the bondage of women to the species'. Woman becomes a 'plaything' of nature, and maternity thus 'dooms' women. De Beauvoir refused to become a mother herself because, I believe, she feared becoming a 'vessel' of nature, condemned to serve 'the species' and not the individual will. Control of her own life was important to her, and she feared that pregnancy would destroy that control.

It could also be said that the mother of modern feminism flunked the greatest and most central challenge of the female condition. Pregnancy is the ultimate test of whether you can maintain a sense of autonomous self while experiencing the condition common to the majority of women. And yet de Beauvoir's calculation was correct in this: she would indeed have lost control of her body, and might have found her mind overwhelmed by feelings she had not necessarily invited.

In pregnancy, there is a gradual and finally irresistible sense that nature is setting the agenda, and that your mind and your rational being are no longer quite your own. Involuntary changes in the taste of food and drink, and in a sense of vulnerability to outside events are experienced: cruelty to small animals can suddenly and spontaneously seem unbearable; the horrors of war, as depicted in TV news reports, unwatchable.

The American feminist Naomi Wolf described her initial, sensible and efficient approach to her first pregnancy when it occurred. She went about making appointments with obstetricians and gynaecologists and calculated the chances for a caesarean. In the third month, she went for an ultrasound scan, as is usual practice, which she again approached in a straightforward, descriptive manner. The technician showed her the pregnancy on the computer screen, coolly scanning for fetal abnormalities, and finding none. 'The spinal cord: see, each vertebra is there. Again, perfect. No visible defect.' Wolf writes that:

'Now the creature assembled itself against the (computer) mouse, manifesting its part seemingly at will, as if it were battering against the membrane between us to make itself blindly known to me. A hand appeared, a forearm, the fist utterly relaxed... A foot, a footprint, white against the blackness, a thin ghostly shank, oddly clumsy toes.

As I saw that hand and that foot, something irrational happened: a lifetime's orientation toward maternal over fetal rights lurched out of kilter. Some voice from the most primitive core of my brain – the voice of the species? – said: *You must protect that little hand at all costs; no harm can come to it or its owner. That little hand, that small human signature, is more important now than you are.* The message was unambivalent.'

This is a persuasive description of the unconscious power of the pregnancy making itself felt.

For Dr Lisa Harris, an assistant professor in the Department of Obstetrics and Gynaecology, writing in the

US journal, *Reproductive Health Matters*, the unconscious power of the pregnancy also gave a powerful prompt. When she was eighteen weeks' pregnant, Dr Harris, an abortion doctor, was carrying out a routine abortion on a patient who was also, coincidentally, eighteen weeks' pregnant. 'I realised that I was more interested than usual in seeing the fetal parts when I was done, since they would so closely resemble those of my own fetus,' she wrote in an academic journal.

'I went about doing the procedure as usual ... I used elec- trical suction to remove the amniotic fluid, picked up my forceps and began to remove the fetus in parts, as I always did. I felt lucky that this one was already in the breech posi- tion – it would make grasping small parts (legs and arms) a little easier. I could see a small foot hanging from the teeth of my forceps. With a quick tug, I separated the leg.

'Precisely at that moment, I felt a kick – a fluttery 'thump, thump' in my own uterus. It was one of the first times I felt fetal movement. There was a leg and foot in my forceps, and a 'thump, thump' in my abdomen. Instantly, tears were streaming from my eyes – without me – meaning, my conscious brain – even being aware of what was going on. I felt as if my response had come entirely from my body, bypassing my usual cognitive processing completely. A message seemed to travel from my uterus to my tear ducts.'

She described it as an 'overwhelming feeling – a brutally visceral response – heartfelt and unmediated by my training or my feminist pro-choice politics.' It was 'one of the raw moments' of her life, and after that, doing second-trimester abortions didn't get any easier, and 'dealing with the little infant parts of my born baby only made dealing with dismembered fetal parts sadder.'

As this exceptionally honest witness attests, nature can indeed 'speak' through the body. And, of course, as pregnancy moves towards birth, the force of nature makes itself felt with overwhelming impact. The onset of labour can have the same effect as a small earthquake: here it comes, and you must go with its flow. Yet, it isn't necessarily an experience of 'bondage' to nature: it can also feel like a kind of partnership that has its own omnipotence.

Prohibition

The 1919 constitutional amendment that introduced the prohibition of all alcohol in the United States (and previously in Finland) was a triumph of feminist crusading. Prohibition was undoubtedly a feminist cause, and strongly linked with suffrage and the vote. From the beginning, the prohibitionists championed suffrage under the common banner of the Women's Christian Temperance Union, and of the first eleven states – all in the west – to endorse the vote, seven became prohibitionist. Feminists campaigned tirelessly – sometimes fanatically – against 'the saloons' with their sometimes debased liquor and loose women. When alcohol was prohibited, sex was, according to one historian, more within women's control.

Active feminist campaigners such as Carrie A. Nation specialised in taking a hatchet to the premises of saloon-owners.

In the early years of prohibition, there were many reports that violence against women (and children) was greatly reduced. Dry states like Utah have consistently maintained lower rates of violent crime, perhaps partly under the control not just of women but of the Mormon Chuch.

Women were always active in temperance movements in Britain and Ireland: working-class women and their children evidently suffered more when men drank (and more, too, when women drank). Temperance music-hall songs were performed by female singers, with such lines as 'Lips that touch liquor will never touch mine', and, from a young girl, 'Sell No More Drink to My Father'. Chicago feminist-prohibitionists carried a banner adorned with the words: 'For the safety of the nation, let the women have the vote/ For the hand that rocks the cradle, will never rock the boat.'

Yet as the 1920s wore on, another kind of woman emerged – the daring gal who danced the Charleston and frequented speakeasies. The poet and wit Dorothy Parker said that prohibition made her a boozer because she loved the transgressive element of illegal drinking. Then again, Dorothy Parker never herself claimed to be a feminist, and perhaps wouldn't have done at a time when feminism was represented by forbidding the joys of the cocktail.

Prostitution

There is a long and honourable tradition of feminist opposition to prostitution: the altogether admirable and heroic Josephine Butler (1828–1906) cared for prostitutes, as well as refugees and victims of slavery, in her own home. Her mission was rooted (as with many nineteenth-century feminists) in her Christian values, and she was an energetic campaigner against the exploitation of underage girls, and the humiliating and often cruel subordination of prostitutes to police health checks. (She was also an effective pioneer of women's education.) Mrs Butler's ideals have come to some fruition in contemporary Swedish legislation against prostitution – led by Swedish feminists – which makes it illegal to buy sexual services, although, perhaps puzzlingly, not to sell the use of one's own body. This seems an attempt to reconcile bodily autonomy – which would allow a person to sell her, or his, own body for use – but halting the sale through organised means, since 'pimping, procuring, rape and operating a brothel' remain illegal.

The Swedish government's position is that prostitution is not to be in any way encouraged by the State, and is indeed to be deplored: 'Prostitution is considered to cause serious harm both to individuals and to society as a whole. Large-scale crime, including human trafficking for sexual purposes, assault, procuring and drug-dealing, is also commonly associated with prostitution. (…)The vast majority of those in prostitution also have very difficult social circumstances.' This position seems to be spreading to Norway, Canada, Northern Ireland and indeed the Irish Republic.

But there are also feminist libertarians who contend that if a person wishes to buy sex, or to sell it, that is their own business. The writer Erica Jong, a feminist libertarian, takes that approach. There is also a school of thought, influenced by liberal economics, that where there is a commercial demand, there will be a supply, and since men desire the bodies of (mainly) young women (and gay men may desire the bodies of young men), that enterprise will always somehow flourish.

It is evident that the trafficking of young persons must always be regarded as wrong, repugnant and illegal. The great journalistic campaigner, W. T. Stead, illustrated by a deliberate action that it was possible to purchase a twelve-year-old girl for prostitution purposes – he was inspired by the actions of Josephine Butler – and raised a nation's conscience on this issue (although even in the 1890s there were libertarians who vehemently objected to his 'meddling' in private morals, including, may I add, my husband's great-grandfather John Addington Symonds – a fierce opponent of Stead's 'meddling', and the Methodist Church's moralising too.) Stead went down in the *Titanic*, and it is said that some libertarians who disliked his 'moralising' lifted a toast: 'To the iceberg!'

But when it comes to adult women (or adult men) selling their bodies for pleasure, problems must arise in forbidding such an exchange. My own inclinations are towards the liberal, but basically uninterested, point of view. What people do in their own bedrooms (or other people's bedrooms) cannot always be regulated by law. We may find some choices unedifying, and we may not wish to have any neighbourly dealings with the activities – few people actually want to live near a brothel, and I have heard those that do often complain about the low ethics of the clientele – but this does not make it a matter, necessarily, of regulation by law.

Feminism champions bodily autonomy – as in, 'I may do what I wish with my own body' – and there is necessarily a conflict here between wanting to outlaw prostitution and allowing adult individuals to make their own choice.

Being a prostitute (or sex-worker, as it is now sometimes called, although new euphemisms usually mean seeking to escape old stigmas) is not a profession most of us would choose for a daughter, niece, god-daughter or grand-daughter, but I have encountered men who say that they have had sex with prostitutes (sex-workers) all their lives, and many of them are just very commercial and, literally, professional women. Commercial, yes: a frequent characteristic of many prostitutes is that they're fond of money, and sensibly, always insist on obtaining the fee before delivering the service. 'Mrs Warren' in George Bernard Shaw's *Mrs Warren's Profession* was a shrewd businesswoman who ran a string of brothels due to the commercial demand (although admittedly her feminist daughter refused to speak to her mother ever again after she discovered the source of the wealth).

Perhaps the Swedish model is the one that will gradually spread throughout the western world. One survey says that about 7.5 per cent of Swedish males bought sex on at least one occasion over a period of a year, so the selling of sex still endures. But then much selling of sex is now done through the internet, so the focus has shifted.

What prostitution, or sex work, does underline, however, is that men and women are different. There are perhaps a few women who purchase the services of rent men, but the demand is seldom voluminous, and the supply-side views it as a little unnecessary, since men infrequently feel the need to sell their services in this regard. The market picture is that men are the buyers, women the sellers – yet another indication that the difference between the genders prevails when it comes to the commerce of sex.

Queens, empresses and aristocrats

It is often affirmed, within the canon of feminism, that feminism should be partnered by socialism, although prominent female socialists were sometimes opposed to feminism. 'Many socialists disapproved of feminism because it sapped energy from consensus about the hegemony of the class struggle,' wrote the biographer of Naomi Mitchison, Scottish novelist and activist.

And the paradox is that women often exercised more power in aristocratic societies than in egalitarian ones. The Byzantine Empire was said never to have been ruled better than under the Empress Theodora. Eleanor of Acquitaine, Blanche of Castile and Catherine de Medici exercised enormous power as queens of France. Isobel of Spain, Elizabeth of England, Catherine the Great of Russia, Tsarina Elisabeth of Russia and Maria Theresa of Austria, were all powerful and accomplished rulers. Queen Victoria in Great Britain defined an entire age, and energised a nation after a series of more or less unsatisfactory kings.

Aristocratic women were chatelaines with responsibilities for great estates, were abbesses (sometimes of joint monasteries), and politically influential through their social networks. Women of rank were often well-educated, as we see from the flowering of female intellectuals in the eighteenth century – the famed 'bluestockings' – whose *salons* helped to develop the intellectual conversations that eventually produced *The Rights of Man* and the French Revolution.

The system of hereditary aristocracy gave women more importance: it came to matter who your mother was, and who your daughter might become. Genealogical lines gave prominence to the mother and father equally, even if formal inheritance was bestowed upon the eldest son, which, today, is increasingly seen as unfair and unequal. European monarchies have now altered their protocols so that the first-born child, of either sex, inherits, and there is some campaigning among the British aristocracy to allow modern families to bestow inheritance, similarly, on the first-born. Demands for feminist equality have now reached the nobility.

Victoria Lambert, a *Daily Telegraph* journalist (and in private life the Countess of Clancarty), is the mother of daughters who has written about the unfairness of this system which favours sons (her husband's title may eventually go to kinsman rather than to their daughters). This question was vividly illustrated after the death of the 6th Duke of Westminster, Gerald Grosvenor. When he died, in 2015, his title and the vast portfolio of property and estates (worth an estimated £8 billion) passed automatically to his son, Hugh, who was his third-born child – the first two being daughters, Lady Tamara and Lady Edwina, who were bypassed.

Is this fair? Victoria Lambert and her supporters think it is not. Daughters should have an equal right to inherit, just as much as sons. They have a case. Although the case for 'equality' among the aristocracy may seem, itself, to be incongruous, since the entire system of hierarchical rank is, by definition, unequal.

Equal rights for posh feminists may not be for the barricades. Historically, aristocracy has often given women many opportunities and advantages seldom enjoyed by their proletarian sisters.

And I'd like to add a personal coda here. The Earl of Clancarty's original title derives from a region in East Galway: The fifth Lord Clancarty is also 'Baron Kilconnell', and my mother's family lived in this region in the 1900s. Lord Clancarty, at that period, had married a beautiful chorus girl, Belle Billson, against his family's wishes, but it was a match that endured, and which provided a narrative of glamour to the countryside. The Countess used to arrive at Hayden's Hotel in Ballinasloe in an exquisite vision of finery, and the local people would line up outside the hotel just to catch a glimpse of her: it was the version of *Hello!* magazine of its time.

But the beautiful Countess developed breast cancer, and her husband, the Earl, nursed her personally until the end of her life, and mourned her ever afterwards. People told stories about the ghost of her carriage being heard through the streets of Ballinasloe on each anniversary of her death.

Nothing whatsoever to do with feminism: yet beauty, and enchantment, and tragic deaths, impart a kind of power, too. The need for stories is as compelling as the desire for equality.

And I'm glad, too, that the earldom of Clancarty has survived into modern generations, and whether daughter or son inherit, may it survive for many more.

Questions, questions: the abortion debate

Abortion is affirmed as a primary right by most mainstream feminists. But it remains a contentious question, and there are women who identify as feminists who uphold the rights for the unborn/ foetus. Here are the main contending viewpoints.

A. Abortion rights are central to feminism, full stop. All contemporary material about feminism affirm abortion as a woman's right over her own body.

> B. There are many women who don't see it as a black-and-white issue. Pro-life feminists trace their roots back to feminist pioneers such as Susan B. Anthony and Elizabeth Cady Stanton, anti-slavery Christians opposed to abortion.

A. That was the nineteenth century and there were other battles to fight. Feminism today means a commitment to choice. You can't be a 'pro-life feminist'.

> B. Hillary Clinton, who campaigned as a pro-choice feminist in the 2016 presidential election, nonetheless said, in the course of that campaign: 'You can certainly be a pro-life feminist. Absolutely.'

A. A woman must have complete sovereignty over her own body. That is what bodily autonomy means. The state or the church should not seek to control a woman's body. That's why we have our placards proclaiming 'my body, my choice'.

B. Yet Ann Furedi, CEO of the British Pregnancy Advisory Service – Britain's largest abortion provider – states in her book *The Moral Case for Abortion*, that 'the status of the foetus cannot easily be set aside'. She concedes that an abortion does involve a 'killing' (though not, for her, of a 'person').

A. Women are people and their status takes priority over that of an embryo or foetus. Women have died, throughout the centuries, because they just did not want a pregnancy, or another pregnancy. Women will still risk death to terminate a pregnancy they do not want.

B. Conditions were often very distressing in an historical context. Over-burdened mothers whose children were already starving; no support; no contraception; and for single women, the stigma of being an unmarried mother which could mean destitution. We can provide better solutions today.

A. It is still up to the woman to decide – nobody else. And for whatever reason she chooses, including a 'wrong-sex' termination. If a woman wants a daughter and finds that her foetus is a male, she should be able to choose to terminate. Dr Wendy Savage, a prominent pro-choice medic, has said that if a woman has a child of an unwanted sex, the child may end up being hated or resented, and she should thus be free to terminate the pregnancy, even if it's a late procedure.

> B. Yet a standard medical textbooks states that 'late abortion can be dangerous and is always disagreeable. The surgical risks rise steeply after twelve to thirteen weeks, the emotional cost to the woman becomes higher and many people feel that the operation becomes more ethically challenging.' Very premature babies are now surviving ever earlier, and there new technologies envisaged in the near future, such as artificial wombs, and biobags that can sustain unborn life.

A. Most abortions are carried out before twelve weeks, and the easier it is to access free abortion, the earlier they can be done. That's why abortion should be easily available and free of charge. The development of the abortion pill is also facilitating more self-administered early termination. Women's equality, her status in society, her ability to conduct a career all require fertility control – and that means abortion as a back-up to contraception. We can judge the status of women in any society according to the freedom allotted to abortion rights.

> B. European societies vary considerably in their abortion rates. In Switzerland, it's 6.3 per thousand women (aged 15 to 44); in Germany, 6.8; in the Netherlands 8.5; while abortion rates in Russia are 32.9, in Bulgaria 21.2 and in Romania 21.2. In Sweden, they are 20.2. Does this mean that in Russia, Bulgaria, Romania and Sweden, women

have more status and equality than in Switzerland, Germany and the Netherlands?

A. There may be other social factors involved in these statistics. Sweden certainly represents a gold standard in women's equality.

B. Indeed, women's choices *may* be often contingent on other factors. Here are some case notes for a batch of second-trimester abortions at a London hospital:

'The patient is twenty weeks pregnant, but the father of her child has left her. She now doesn't want the pregnancy.'

'The patient has lost her job so cannot benefit from maternity leave.'

'The patient is still at school – she concealed her pregnancy until her mother found out. She has agreed to a termination.'

'This patient is twenty-three weeks pregnant and has been made homeless. She has decided she cannot continue the pregnancy.'

These destructive operations were occasioned by social problems which we could alleviate.

A. By all means, we should give women every economic option and social support. Feminists have always fought for better conditions for women with wanted pregnancies – feminists have fought for maternity allowances, for maternity leave, for childcare, for nurseries, and for access to assisted conception. But we must still maintain the principle that it is a woman's free choice, and she is in the best position to consider her circumstances. Trust women's judgement.

B. But what about doctors (or nurses) who dissent? In Italy, 70 per cent of doctors are now refusing, on grounds of conscience, to carry out routine abortions (up from 58 per cent in 2005).

A. The European Committee on Social Rights, part of the Council of Europe, has condemned the Italian situation as being a violation of women's rights and 'protection of health'. By the same token, the United Nations has condemned Ireland for submitting women to 'torture' by not providing abortion rights, and for its constitutional pledge to protect the foetus.

B. In Ireland, constitutional rights are subject to referendum, so it comes down to a democratic decision as to what kind of law the people wish to have in their country. Trust the people!

A. In Catholic countries, the power of the Catholic Church is often an influential element. That's why we have a slogan 'Keep your rosaries off our ovaries.'

B. Shouldn't that be updated to 'let's have a ban – on the ultrascan?' It's the techniques of the ultrasound scan and developments in embryology and fetology that are modernising this debate. Note how in popular films like *Bridget Jones's Baby*, the ultrasound scan of the unborn is so central to establishing the baby as a real presence in the scenario, even very early on.

A. Babies are cute, but it is still up to the woman as to whether she wants a child. That must be the solid and unchanging feminist position. What Stella Browne said in 1935 is still universally upheld by the feminist movement: 'Abortion should be available for any woman, without insolent inquisitions, nor ruinous financial charges, nor tangles of red tape. For our bodies are our own.'

B. Yet, opinion polls among women show far more nuances, and many more 'mixed feelings'. 70 per cent of British women would like the current abortion time-limit reduced, 93 per cent of women would like to see independent pre-abortion counselling, 91 per cent want sex-selection abortions banned and 84 per cent want improved pregnancy support for women in crisis. The unborn is recognised as a life.

A. It's simple: feminism must be defined as pro-choice.

B. Some of us would define ourselves as feminists for life.

Rape

As we know, rape is an odious crime, which should always be reported to the police, and, where there is evidence, should always be prosecuted. The problem with reporting rape is the complications that come with evidence.

If someone commits a burglary, an embezzlement, a homicide, or an assault of actual, or grievous, bodily harm, the criminal prosecution depends on evidence and witnesses. With rape, there is usually no other witness. And where the burden of proof depends on 'consent', it can get particularly complicated, especially since sexual signals can be non-verbal. ('Ma! He's making eyes at me!') But since males (in general) are physically stronger than females, and since females cannot (usually) rape males, it is not unreasonable that we should think of women as being in the more vulnerable situation, and that the law should act protectively towards females as victims. Women's statements were sometimes not believed in the past, or not taken seriously, or they were judged according to their moral character, which often resulted in injustice and in rapists walking free. In wartime, women were systematically raped and suffered dreadfully, and yet the history books have mostly been silent about it. (*Downfall*, Anthony Beevor's account of German women raped by the

Soviet Armies in 1945 gives a pitiful account of wartime rape – and the silence that subsequently surrounded it.)

Susan Brownmiller's 1975 book, *Against Our Will*, was an awakening on the issue of rape, although her claim that rape was more to do with power than with sex is not universally accepted. Sometimes it is quite evidently about sex, or sex coercively subjected to physical power.

Camille Paglia has written robustly about women using common sense and being aware of the dangers of putting themselves in risky situations: she claims that by rigidly insisting on the equality of the sexes, feminism has hidden the truth from young women. 'Feminism keeps saying the sexes are the same. It keeps telling women they can do anything, go anywhere, say anything, wear anything. No, they can't.' The feminist view of sex is 'naïve and prudish'. In groups, she warns, young men are dangerous. 'A woman going to a fraternity [college] party is walking into Testosterone Flats, full of prickly cacti and blazing guns. She should arrive with girlfriends and leave with them. A girl who lets herself get dead-drunk at a fraternity party is a fool. A girl who goes upstairs alone with a [man] at a fraternity party is an idiot. Feminists call this "blaming the victim". I call it common sense.'

Rape is a crime, she insists. But sex is 'nature's red flame', which must be tamed. 'Generation after generation, men must be educated, refined and ethically persuaded away from their tendency towards anarchy and brutishness.' Quite so.

Rape and alcohol

A female High Court judge on the eve of retirement, presiding over a rape case, decided to give some general advice to young women, just as she would – she reflected later – to a daughter.

Judge Lindsey Kushner QC, aged sixty-five, at her final trial at Manchester Crown Court, jailed the accused, Ricardo Rodrigues-Gomes, aged nineteen, to six years in jail for raping Megan Clark, also a teenager, by a canalside.

Speaking at the end of the trial, Judge Kushner (herself the mother of a daughter and a son), said that while women were 'perfectly entitled to drink themselves into the ground' if they chose, nevertheless, they should be aware that in that state, potential rapists might gravitate towards them. If intoxicated, such women would be less likely to report the rape, and less likely to be able to remember the details. 'I don't think it's wrong for a judge to beg women to take actions to protect themselves,' she said. You wouldn't leave the back door of your house open at night, she said, to invite burglars in. If burglars did enter, it wouldn't make their crime any the less: but a householder might still be expected to take common-sense precautions.

Mrs Kushner was met with a storm of protest at these utterances. She was accused of 'blaming the victim'. She was criticised by women's charity campaigners and by one of Britain's senior police and crime commissioners, Dame Vera Baird QC.

Subsequently, however, the actual victim of that rape crime, Megan Clark, then herself nineteen, said that the judge was right to make her point. Ms Clark had been drinking lager and vodka on that night, and had inhaled the party drug amyl nitriate before she was attacked, wrote Gabriella Swerling in *The Times*, in a retrospective interview with Judge Kushner. Because of the blur caused by boozing, Megan said she would probably not have reported the rape if another witness hadn't filmed it on a mobile phone. (It was played in court and clinched the conviction.)

Lindsey Kushner, who was called to the bar in 1974, became very concerned at what she called the 'explosion' of rape and sexual assault charges that she had seen in the last twenty years of her time on the bench. And it was evident to her that alcohol was often involved in the events preceding the crime.

A lot more could, and should, be done in education for both males and females, and society at large, Mrs Kushner said. People shouldn't be too shy to intervene if they saw someone 'starting on some woman inappropriately – at whatever level – whether being verbally abusive or touching inappropriately all the way through to rape, and say, "don't you dare".'

Men shouldn't think that 'because a woman dresses or behaves in a certain way, or is drinking, that this gives them a licence to try and have sex with them – whether they may want it or they may not'.

And when she sees girls out on the town, sometimes, 'I worry about them. When the clubs are coming out or something like that, if they're the worse for wear for drink, I worry about them. And … as far as violence is concerned, things blow up within seconds, so drink has some bearing on that.'

Does drink have some bearing on all that? As our learned friends say: *res ipsis loquitor.* *

*The question answers itself.

Reproductive rights – or aspirations?

Fertility can be unpredictable. My mother married at twenty-three, had a miscarriage at twenty-five, a baby at twenty-six, two more babies subsequently, and then (without recourse to contraception), ten years of what she called 'normal married life' without a pregnancy. Then, in her forties, she surprisingly – and to her great annoyance – conceived again. That was me. My father was sixty-seven and delighted. Ma could never figure out why she could go a decade without a pregnancy, and then have it happen.

The medical specialists are aiming to make fertility an exact science so that those who do not want babies shall not have them, and those who do want babies shall have them. Contraception was a major focus in the twentieth century; in the twenty-first, the more exciting project has been the extension of fertility. An immense degree of human hope and striving continues to be invested in the achievement of fertility: this was powerfully illuminated, for me, in a play I saw (at London's Park Theatre) about a couple's struggles with IVF, called *The Quiet House*, written by Gareth Farr, and drawing directly on his own experience.

This is the story of Dylan and Jess, both thirty-four, who are undergoing in vitro fertilisation in an increasingly strained effort to have a baby. The emotions and the stress are played out before us: belief, despair, conflict, pain, loss, and indeed drama.

An alarm clock ticks on stage, as well as internally, as the couple wait two minutes to see if the egg (or eggs) has been fertilised and if their pregnancy test is positive. When it registers 'no pregnancy', it is a terrible blow, and the couple's attempt at cheerfulness turns to a howling rage.

As many who have undergone IVF attest, it's no fun having sex to order, at exactly the right moment when fertility is at its peak. And, as Dylan bursts out in anger and frustration at one point, he sees himself as little more than, literally, 'a wanker'. 'I have no part in this,' he shouts, utterly exhausted with the whole process. 'I wank. That's what I do. That's how you described my part in all this.' The husband then seems less committed to the process: 'We have one another,' he pleads. Isn't that enough? He's under pressure at work and doesn't want to disclose to colleagues the daily drama at home. Dylan needs his wife's constant reassurance, especially when he calls himself 'a Jaffa – seedless.' They love and hug and fight and shout at each other: he administers her painful stomach injections that should boost her egg potential. There's a neighbour with a baby, and the sight of the infant in her mother's arms is as painful to Jess as any number of needles into her stomach. There are five embryos in the lab waiting re-implantation in Jess's womb. Then there are three, as two perish, or 'become unviable', as the jargon puts it. When alone, Jess talks to the embryo (an embryo is a conceptus up to eight weeks). 'I know you. You. Your personality and I know your sense of humour. I do. I know your love … I know your love and I will know your face. I will know your voice.' When the embryos perish, the preciousness of a pregnancy so ardently wanted is overpowering. They're in grief. Jess's desire for a baby is eloquently, even desperately expressed. 'I want a baby … I want one more than you could possibly ever imagine. More than I thought I could ever want anything. So much so that it hurts me. It causes me actual physical pain....' Do they succeed in achieving a pregnancy? They almost feel they can't face another IVF cycle, and then try one more time, and at the end, we are left in suspension as the clock ticks once more. In real life, the story turned out happily for Gareth Farr and his wife Gabby Vautier when they had twin daughters after a gruelling experience of IVF. Like many couples, they had had 'unexplained infertility' – there was no evident reason why they had not conceived in the course of nature. They hadn't been prepared for what Gareth has described as the embarrassment, the invasion of privacy, the stressful impact on their relationship, and for many couples, the cost. In an era when we talk about gender equality and the fluidity of sexual identity, it can be a shock to couples to realise that although conception should be a shared experience, in IVF the focus, is on the woman and her body. The whole drama of nature takes place within a woman's body: it may be claimed that a woman is in charge of her own anatomy, but with IVF, her body becomes a laboratory of both nature and science. All the man has to do is produce the sperm, and after that he may feel redundant and uncertain about what's expected from him. *The Quiet House* is so called because the couple feel their home is too quiet without babies. But do this gilded young duo expect too much? They've been accustomed to the idea that they have 'the right to choose', and it's perhaps difficult to accept that nature does not always award choices. Wanting something desperately does not always mean getting it. Medical science can help, but it can't always provide a remedy.

A young couple I know of went through three cycles of IVF to much anguish and no outcome. They gave up the process, and then suddenly, when the woman was forty, a pregnancy occurred naturally and a precious baby daughter was born. A few years on, and the same woman has unexpectedly had a second baby. As my ma discovered, first to her fury, and afterwards to her pleasure, nature can still pop a surprise, and with all our advances, fertility is still not a mathematically exact science.

'Reproductive rights' can be affirmed but not guaranteed: a 'right' to conceive and have a child may be enhanced, but no law can be certain to deliver it. Sandeep and Reena Mander, a British Sikh couple seeking to adopt, had been through sixteen cycles of in vitro fertilisation, without success. Where were their 'reproductive rights'? As Ann Furedi (of the British Pregnancy Advisory Service) has written: 'Fertility is one of the things that we cannot control entirely. Even today, it is not possible to plan to become pregnant on schedule. For many women, it is impossible to get pregnant at all despite the greater availability of, and advances in, assisted reproductive technologies.' Precisely: no agency can deliver 'reproductive rights'. A stand-up female comedian in the United States unwittingly illustrated this with an 'edgy' feminist joke. 'I really want to have an abortion,' she said. 'But my boyfriend and I are having trouble getting pregnant!' She had to apologise for the quip after a storm of protests, mostly from women who really were trying to get pregnant (who also found it insulting that they would terminate a much-wanted pregnancy). It certainly was offensive, but with its paradoxical wisecrack, it illustrated the point that 'reproductive rights' can never be guaranteed, and it is therefore false to claim such rights.

Science

One of the greatest scientists of the twentieth century – to whom we owe innovations in cancer treatment – was a woman, Marie Curie (who also worked with her daughter, Yvonne Jolie-Curie). But there is continuing discontent amongst us due to the fact that women have not achieved anything like parity in the science fields. 'Why are so few women publishing scientific papers?' asked Jenny Gristock in *The Guardian* while referring to an article in *New Scientist* magazine. Ms Gristock writes that we need more women in science, but the problem is that there is still gender bias in this field: a study in the *American Economic Review* showed that women suffered earning's penalties in science if they have children, while male scientists do not:

> 'European social science research shows that male and female scientists often have different types of partners: male scientists more frequently have a stay-at-home partner looking after the children, while female scientists are more likely to have another scientist as a spouse. So male scientists might not need family-friendly working practices to have a successful career, but female scientists do. Hence the loss of women in the "leaky pipeline" of scientific careers.'

There's another prejudice too: scientists perceived job applicants to be less competent when they had female names.

A House of Commons committee concluded that encouraging schoolgirls to go into a career in science is not enough. 'Efforts are wasted if women are subsequently disproportionately disadvantaged in scientific careers compared to men.' The journal, *Science*, asked whether it was 'too much to ask women in science organistions to change misogynistic culture in a world that remains misogynistic'.

Evidently, science needs to sharpen up its gender-equality act and inspire and support more girls and women in the field. And maybe female scientists should consider not mating with male scientists, but seek out some home-based male novelist, say, who would be happier to be a house-husband working from home.

Discrimination and prejudice are unacceptable, but still, freedom to choose will play some part in gender roles. A group of teenage girls studied by David Lubinski and Camilla Benbow, who were encouraged by parents to study science (they were sent to a special summer school to develop their science and mathematic abilities) nevertheless said that they were more interested in people, in 'social values' and altruistic and humanitarian goals than in pure science and maths, whereas the boys who were their peers preferred science and maths. Less than 1 per cent of these young women who showed an aptitude (and had parental encouragement) chose maths, engineering or the physical sciences at university; they preferred law, medicine, biology and the humanities – all subjects that deal with people.

Women commonly outnumber men in university intake, and in biological sciences like medicine this is particularly notable. But as careers develop, there are always fewer women in the fields of science and engineering. The social scientist Patti Hausman has suggested that personal choice is a significant factor in this: 'The question of why more women don't choose careers in engineering has a rather obvious answer: because they don't want to. Wherever you go, you will find females far less likely than males to see what is so fascinating about ohms, carburettors or quarks.'

This is not a widely accepted view – prejudice, misogyny and the 'glass ceiling' are more usually blamed. But a genuinely scientific approach would be to keep an open mind on the causes, and continue to examine the evidence.

Sexual Consent Law

Frances Fitzgerald announced in January 2017, when she occupied the position of Minister for Justice and Equality, that she would bring legislation before the Oireachtas (the Irish parliament) to define and clarify sexual consent.

The intention is excellent, and has been striven for in codes of conduct throughout the centuries, from the chivalric efforts during the Renaissance to instil 'gentlemanliness', to the Victorians stigmatising a seducer as a 'cad and a bounder'. The Don Juans who 'took advantage' of women were always deplored by civilised society, and rightly so. (Even so, more than one cad and bounder got away with his exploits, leaving many a ruined woman, literally, holding the baby.)

Today, the law is tending to replace manners and morals of yore by redefining this sphere of behaviour in legal terms. But can the law always define what 'consent' really means in a sexual relationship? Yes, if there is blatant evidence of rape or assault. And intoxication or drug-addled unconsciousness should be no defence against rape or assault. It may not be edifying if a woman is too drunk to know (or remember) what is going on, but sexual intimacy in these circumstances is still a wrongful act.

It's when we get into more complex and subtle areas that 'consent' becomes difficult to define in law. The law depends on evidence of what is said and what is done: the law cannot easily deal with the secret signals of the heart and the eyes, which may be interpreted in any which way.

Shakespeare explains all this, with his customary insight into human nature and finesse of language, in *The Merchant of Venice*, when Bassanio says of Portia: 'Sometimes from her eyes I did receive fair speechless messages.'

And popular music is full of allusions to non-verbal messages that imply seduction or desire. The Everly Brothers had a great song that begins: 'What do you want to make those eyes at me for?/ When they don't mean what they say?' The lyrics of this hit could even be interpreted as a threat of rape: the girl to whom the song is addressed is told she is 'fooling around' with the boy, that she's 'leading him on'. She is warned that she's going to find that she's 'messing with dynamite' when he 'gets her alone some night'.

How, exactly, would Minister Fitzgerald, or any legislature, translate the myriad messages of flirtation, emotional engagement, desire, and even lust, into a fair and satisfactory law? 'It is impossible,' wrote Simone de Beauvoir, 'to bring the sexual instinct under a code of regulation.' The law cannot control all intercourse between individuals, and were it to try, we would call it totalitarianism. Minister Fitzgerald must have experienced a certain relief when a political reshuffle changed her brief, and the challenge of defining and clarifying sexual consent in all human exchanges now passes to her successor.

Sexual revolution:
the genesis

I was writing a weekly column for the *Sunday Telegraph* back in the 1980s when I received a letter from a man called 'Paddy' O'Connor (his real name was Anthony, but he was known as 'Paddy'); he said that something I had written interested him, and he wanted to talk to me about his memory of being involved in an organisation called The World League for Sexual Reform when he was a young lad in the 1930s. Paddy had an Irish name, but he was a Scot, and he lived with his wife – his children were grown and flown – in a pleasant London suburb. I thought his letter was interesting and I set off to meet him on a sunny Saturday afternoon.

We met up and went to a café for tea and cake. He was a genial old chap, and he evidently wanted to pass on to someone younger his recollections of those pioneering days. I must have written something that stimulated his interest, and he wanted to tell me about his attachment, back in the 1930s, to that aforementioned organisation (The World League for Sexual Reform). This organisation was led by a flamboyant Australian gynaecologist called Norman Haire, himself a disciple of another colourful German gynaecologist called Magnus Hirschfeld (whose works were banned and burned by the Nazis.) Much of what Norman Haire advocated was considered very advanced at the time: homosexual rights (he was a homosexual), birth control, abortion, sex education and legalised prostitution.

Dr Haire was supported in his endeavours by the progressive luminaries of the time, including Dora Russell (wife of Bertrand) and Naomi Mitchison, the accomplished Scottish writer, socialist and eugenicist, a sister of the equally progressive J. B. S. Haldene (some might consider it 'patriarchal' to mention a woman's connection to a male relative, only Naomi Mitchison herself was very keen on eugenic links and proud to be associated with the clever and eccentric Haldene clan).

Paddy recalled that golden time: 'I loved it because it was so new, so exciting.' It was all so different from the ambience of his stable, but dull, family life. Everything spoken at the World League for Sexual Reform seemed utterly outrageous to respectable bourgeois society. Naomi Mitchison – who Paddy worshipped – had written a book on birth control which even Victor Gollancz, the courageous left-wing publisher, refused to publish in the 1940s as it would surely have caused a scandal. Mrs Mitchison advanced free love, enjoyed the benefits of an open marriage, and was the mother of seven children (as the Haldenes were so intelligent, they felt they deserved to proliferate their genes).

He spoke about all this with the pleasure of recollection. Was he himself a sexual radical, I asked? Look, he repeated, the ideas were such a novelty, so stimulating, that he couldn't but be carried along. It was all so exciting! As he spoke, I remembered just how I felt when I first encountered the Women's Liberation Movement in New York in 1967: it was all so exhilarating! So thrilling to be part of a small, radical group that outraged the respectable classes.

The World League for Sexual Reform was a very small group indeed in the 1930s, and very much outside the boundaries of respectable society – even the progressive Bloomsburies didn't want to be publicly associated – so there was a piquant feeling of secrecy to the meetings that Paddy greatly relished. Norman Haire was something of an eccentric, but he was also quite wealthy, and often appeared in ostentatious motor cars. He had a Harley Street practice offering 'rejuvenation' therapy to older people: among his clients was the poet W. B. Yeats. The therapy was subsequently regarded as rather bogus – it was little more than a vascectomy. And yet, Haire had pre-empted the idea of Viagra, or at least profitably anticipated the market for it.

Paddy told me stories about the people he encountered at the World League meetings: a very impressive woman who astonished him – as a young lad at the time – by carrying around contraceptives in her handbag and daringly producing them when the conversation turned to free love. But life doesn't always turn out as planned, he mused. Later, when she wanted children, she discovered she couldn't conceive and was devastated – though she did successfully adopt the child of a woman who hadn't been prudent enough to carry around a contraceptive in her own handbag.

Some of the World League attendees were also Communists with much admiration for the Soviet Union, where they imagined a kind of Utopia had been attained. Stella Browne, who coined the phrase, 'the right to choose', was a noted 'militant Communist' who was also a feminist.

Paddy produced some of the World League pamphlets from a bag and gave them to me. They were modest little productions: the organisation was clearly not exactly mainstream. And yet, every idea that Norman Haire put forward eventually entered mainstream culture and, it might be said, entirely conquered respectable society.

The World League crossed over with feminists among radicals like Naomi Mitchison and Dora Russell, but mainstream feminists at the time distinguished between feminism and sexology. Feminists like Vera Brittain were supportive of birth control in a dignified and discreet way, to help the health of mothers, but they considered the ideas of Hirschfeld and Haire 'extreme'. Stella Browne warned colleagues that it would endanger gradual reform of abortion laws to be seen as too radical. Yet, not all left-wing feminists were in favour of birth control: Rosa Luxembourg opposed contraception.

Germaine Greer was to point out, later in the century, that the sexual revolution and the feminist revolution were not the same, even though they had points in common and were sometimes conflated. Some feminists came to see the sexual revolution of the 1960s as essentially exploitative of women – and to the advantage of men.

Paddy O'Connor and I had a pleasant talk, and a very lively one. I pressed him on certain points, as is routine with a journalistic interview. And then we parted on friendly terms and he said he had some household shopping to do at the local supermarket.

Later in the day, when I was back at home, I received a call from his wife. She was ringing to ask me if I was still with Paddy, as he hadn't returned after our meeting. I told her we'd parted and he had gone off to do his shopping. She was puzzled and concerned. Subsequently, I received a call from another member of his family saying that Paddy had

had a sudden heart attack in the supermarket and had died immediately.

In some way, I felt vaguely responsible. Perhaps all the recollections of those heady times in the World League for Sexual Reform had excited him and the ensuing palpitations caused a cardiac arrest. Perhaps I had prompted some cardiac arousal with all this talk of sexual liberation? Older men do die in such circumstances.

Anyway, he had wanted to transmit his memories and donate his leaflets from the World League for Sexual Reform, and I still have them. Since they seemed to represent the most thrilling time of his life, perhaps it was a fitting moment for death, after all.

Soldier women

I am sitting next to a lieutenant-colonel from the British Ministry of Defence at a dinner party. So I ask him the question I always like to ask military personnel: 'Should women serve as front-line soldiers in armies?'

A hesitation. It is now policy that women should serve on an equal basis with men. The Lieutenant-Colonel did a wavering mime with his hand. 'I have my reservations,' he said in a half-embarrassed way.

'Which are?'

'Soldiers' bodies take a hell of a beating. In older years, they often end up in a pretty bad state. You can't imagine the amount of gear that the infantry has to carry.' He obviously didn't like the thought of women's bodies being subjected to the same punishment.

'But isn't it a woman's choice whether her body ends up in a hell of a mess or not?'

'Yes, that's the idea,' he smiled. But he wasn't comfortable with it.

'What about those ace Kurdish women fighters?'

'Ah yes. Indeed. Remarkable.'

'And the female snipers in the Soviet Army during the Second World War? They were terrific.'

'The sniper's role is a very particular one. It depends on patience.'

Indeed, the Russians recruited around one million women to serve in various branches of the military from 1941 onwards, and trained 400,000 young women to become snipers. Female patience was often offered as a reason for women's suitability: Lyudmila Pavlichenko, the champion female sniper known as a 'warrior princess' was apparently able to maintain a stationary position, lying in mud and water, for twenty-four hours.

These Soviet women snipers showed enormous courage and endurance; some had terrible deaths: some were tortured and hanged by the enemy. Some were raped – by their own male comrades. Beautiful ballet dancers lost their legs.

They lived through incredibly tough experiences, and yet, there is often a feminine note to the stories, as so poignantly told by Lyuba Vinogradova. The Cossack girls wept bitterly when they had to have their plaits cut off. One particular sharpshooter, Tonya Bulanenko, had a terrific eye and a steady aim, but she just 'couldn't shoot at people'.

They usually operated in twos, and formed deep and meaningful bonds with their sniping partners. Some grieved for the rest of their lives for a sniping partner who had died during the war.

There is a feminist view – suggested by the psychologist Carol Milligan – that women are innately nurturing and peaceful and thus not orientated towards serving in a war machine. Some of the Russian snipers did have that reflex after their first kill. Tonya Makhlyagina shot a German who appeared above a parapet. 'She saw him fall. Her delight took her breath away. She had hit the target! But she was immediately crushed by a terrible thought: "That was somebody's father and I have killed him!"' The German had a moustache and was middle-aged, which was why she surmised he might be 'somebody's father'. She was an orphan herself, and now she felt she may have orphaned other children. He had not fired first. She burst into tears. Other women had that appalled reflex too. 'I've killed a person!'

But war hardens, and Hitler's invasion of Russia was brutal. The fighting women began to see the target not as 'a German … a father', but 'the enemy'.

The women fought as hard as any man. And yet, people didn't always react well afterwards, and the survivors weren't always treated well. Some were accused of being 'front-line wives' to the male soldiers. Some suffered guilt and what we would now called post-traumatic stress disorder. This also happens to many men on the battlefield.Some did remake their lives (and the ballet-dancer whose legs were shattered was able to teach at the Bolshoi for many years afterwards).

They were officially praised in 1945, but they were also told not to forget their 'primary duty to nation and State – that of motherhood.' One of the ace snipers, Anya Mulatova, struggled with poverty and housing difficulties, and had to abandon her post-war studies when her husband, who was drinking heavily, accused her of not keeping the house tidy.

Women surely can fight as well as men: but it's possible that their approach to military engagement isn't always the same. The Soviet women placed great emphasis on 'defending the Motherland' – that motivation was important. For Kurdish women, they are defending their tribe.

If some military men are ambivalent about women serving as equals, some are opposed to it. Colonel Richard Kemp, who commanded the British forces in Afghanistan in 2003, esteems women as combat pilots, medics, engineers and fire controllers. 'I have had many women under my command on operations and can vouch for their courage and effectiveness, which have been every bit as great as any man's,' he has written. And yet, he claims that it's hard for women to 'fit into this testosterone-charged band of brothers,' which demands a 'warrior ethos'. Men, he says, are simply more aggressive than women, and when it comes to the infantry, attacking an enemy and perhaps killing him face to face 'with bullets, bayonets, grenades, and if necessary, in hand-to-hand combat' is not likely to appeal to many women.

The military author, Sir Max Hastings, regards the question of women serving on an equal basis with men as:

'A complex one. Rationally there remains a good argument against having women in the front line. The old argument spelt out by Charles Guthrie, among others, was "you cannot leave a woman behind on the battlefield". The real objection, supported by innumerable scientific surveys on both sides of the Atlantic, is that women's endurance and load-carrying capabilities are not the same as men's.

'Nonetheless, I have changed my own mind on this issue. I was always against women on the front line for the above reasons. But the armed forces have to move with the spirit of the times and reflect the mood of civilian society. I think it is now inevitable that women should serve in the front line, even if few wish to do so, as current generals tell me they think is the case. To put the matter bluntly, and as also tested by homicide statistics, women have a much stronger psychological response to killing people, the fundamental job of soldiers, and long may that continue to be the case.'

But let us turn to the experience of a woman officer who has served (with the British troops) in Afghanistan, and elsewhere, and allow her to give a vivid, honest and knowledgeable account on serving and fighting alongside men:

'There are two very different issues here – 'serving' and 'fighting'. The first is relatively easy – I absolutely accept that women can and should serve on an equal basis with men in armies. In my experience there are different qualities which different genders will bring to an army – the most common and often observed are risk-taking (men) and fact-checking / diligence (women). I know this is an enormous generalisation, but I have observed it countless times – and I think the military reinforces stereotypes, making them more prevalent. Both these qualities need tempering – we probably need more women in banking, if it comes to that.

'Fighting is more complex. Physiologically, it's true that women are of course different to men. As a result, the Personal Fitness Assessment each member of the army must take twice a year has different pass / fail categories for men and women (women have to do twenty-one press-ups in two minutes, men forty-four). As female officers we were expected to do forty-four, but I met plenty who did not. That this standard remains seems to me a pretty clear indicator of the awareness of different physical strength levels.

'There is a minimum level of physical strength required in order to fight. It is worth explaining why this is – a soldier involved in combat needs sufficient strength to carry their equipment to a position where they can fight from; a ballpark figure for a soldier's load would be 60 kg. There are fewer women who are capable of carrying this load for a long distance over difficult terrain. That doesn't mean that some women aren't physically able to carry out the same tasks to the appropriate standard. I believe such women should absolutely be allowed to fight on an equal basis with men in armies. The risk is that the standard could be lowered in order to allow apparent equality. There's also another related issue here which is that of physical endurance over a period of years – the women who are fit and strong enough to pass the initial training may deteriorate more quickly than their male counterparts.

'Then, sexually, there's an issue. War zones are notoriously emotional places – I'm sure there's a statistic somewhere about more babies being born in war. Anyway, this is a genuine issue which needs to be dealt with. But if we allow gay men to fight, which of course we do, it's difficult for the military to come up with a justification for not allowing straight women to do so.

'However, a relationship within a small unit, at war, is a very dangerous thing – it means peoples' minds are not absolutely focused on the task at hand.

'One of the things that all infantry units do before deploying is a welfare interview to establish whether the soldiers have personal, family, or financial worries. They do this so that the soldier can focus. If his girlfriend is on patrol with him, there is definitely a risk.

'It's a commonly held view that a female soldier's presence can change the dynamic in a platoon. I certainly noticed that soldiers far junior to me were always checking I was okay on patrols, when they should perhaps have been checking their arcs of fire, or scanning the ground for signs of IEDs. (Improvised Explosive Device, e.g. nail bombs.) I suppose that this is something which would eventually change, but in the immediate term, it can affect operational effectiveness. A large proportion of our soldiers come from deprived backgrounds in which women hold much more traditional roles, which I feel would slow this change.

'How many women want to fight alongside men? I think it's worth recognising that this is actually more of an issue for feminists than it is for women in the military (although of course we can be feminists too!). Of my platoon of thirty, I would guess that a maximum of seven would have wanted to join the infantry. Of these, I expect only four would have been able to pass the infantry battle course due to its physical demands. The injured platoon at Sandhurst was always disproportionately full of women. And of course, being in the infantry when things go wrong is the worst place to be on earth, so I always have a slightly grim laugh at the masses of women determined to allow that their sisters too can be blown up, shot and traumatised just as much as men can.'

Women can be extraordinarily valiant in combat, and as part of the defence forces, on land, sea and air (women were pioneering aviators from the earliest flying days). A professional army needs female skills – computer technology, mathematical ability and algorhithms are as important today as raw weaponry. But a fifty-fifty distribution in soldiering is unlikely to happen in any of our lifetimes.

'Sluts and Prudes'

(1) SlutWalks

The 'SlutWalk' was a protest movement that started in Canada in 2011 (after a Toronto policeman, Michael Sanguinetti, advised women against 'dressing like sluts' – he subsequently apologised), and for the next three or four years there were 'SlutWalks' all over the globe. These were marches against 'rape culture' and against the idea of 'blaming the victim' (for wearing provocative clothes, or few clothes at all, and 'inviting' an assault).

It can be an imaginative gesture to repossess and 'own' a word that was originally intended as an insult. After Hillary Clinton called Trump voters 'deplorables', some of the said voters affirmed themselves defiantly as Hillary's 'deplorables', thus turning the concept against the originator (who was thus made to realise that she had made a tactical error). 'Queer' was a somewhat disparaging word used about homosexuals back in the 1940s and 50s (and before): gay men and women in recent times have sought to repossess it with pride – the Tate Gallery in London ran a highly successful exhibition about gay artists called 'Queer Art'. Repossession had also been carried out in military engagements: the British Expeditionary Force in the First World War was described as 'a contemptible little army' by Kaiser Wilhelm – and after that the BEF nicknamed themselves 'the Old Contemptibles'. England cricket fans were disparagingly described by the Australian media in the 1990s as 'a barmy army', and they embraced the soubriquet.

The most successful repossession of all was the very word 'Suffragette', which was bestowed upon the British women suffragettes in the early 1900s by a scoffing popular press. They took it and ran with it, and made it into something brilliant, honourable and historically unforgettable.

So why not repossess and redefine the word 'slut', used disparagingly about women? The SlutWalks were, for a time, successful in raising issues over blaming women when sexual assault or harassment took place. And yet, it was a slightly risky strategy, as all irony can be, particularly when it strays into the arena of sexual politics. There are too many people who take words literally, and even some women saw the 'SlutWalk' movement as demeaning rather than affirmative.

The word itself has some ambiguity for me. When I was growing up, a 'slut' quite often meant a careless or feckless housekeeper (when the word was sometimes associated, or even doubled up with, 'slattern'.) The slut is the woman who can't be bothered to wash the dishes, vacuum or springclean, and who'd as soon put up with a messy house than spend her day attending to it. Many is the time I was called a slut myself, and many's the time I have been a slut (and a slattern); I might even say I've been proud of my sluttishness. By that, I don't necessarily mean walking through the streets in a state of undress and gaudy make-up (though I'm sure I did that too): but, rather, choosing to lie in bed reading a book rather than apply myself to the housewifely chores that might await.

Back in the 1960s, the columnist Katharine Whitehorn wrote a famous piece – which cheered us all up greatly

– about the joys of being a slut. It contained such gems of advice as how to pick the least-soiled piece of underwear from the laundry basket when we've been too idle to do our washing, and, in the days of suspender belts for stockings, using an aspirin where the missing bobble should be. Set against a women's-magazine culture that emphasised 'good housekeeping' and the absolute necessity of wearing immaculately white gloves at garden parties, it was a tonic. But it had little to do with low sexual morals.

(2) Prudes

What do I know about sexting and selfies among young people? Nothing. So, with permission, I will invite a younger writer, Laura Freeman, to take the witness box. 'What advice would you give to this modern moral question posed by my friend's younger sister?' she asks in an article in *The Spectator*.

> 'A boy at school had asked her to send him a selfie. Nude, naturally. She was dithering. She liked the boy, a sixth-form crush, and was keen to endear herself. But she knew that if she sent a naked picture he'd pass it on to his friends. She had thought of compromises: just her breasts, or her bottom coyly reflected in a mirror. It hadn't crossed her mind to say "get lost". Then, she explained, he'd tell his friends she was a prude. That, to her, was far worse than the First XI seeing her in the nuddy…
>
> I don't know what my pal's sister decided. I gave her the full treatment: "Just say no", "Your body, your rules", and "Love means never having to send a belfie (a bottom selfie). I said the only way to stop

naked pictures being leaked, hacked and pinned to the common-room noticeboard was not to take them in the first place.

And what's so bad about being a prude, anyway? Let's reclaim "prude". Turn it from a male insult to an empowering hashtag: #JeSuisPrude. We should be proud to be prudes. To say "No, thank you, I'd rather not."

I'm weary of having to be "OK" about everything. Yeah, I'm cool with pole-dancing classes at the gym. Yeah, I'm cool with Kim Kardashian's Brazilian wax. Yeah, I'm cool with an open relationship. Yeah, I'm cool with the picturesque, candlelit rape scenes on Sunday-night TV dramas. Yeah, I'm cool with stag-do trips to strip clubs: "Off you go, darling, have a lovely time."

But I'm not cool with any of it. Nor are most of my girlfriends, all of us in our late twenties. We came of age in the naughty Noughties with sexting and YouPorn and Tinder, and we're supposed to be super-liberal and up for anything. Some go along with it, repressing the inner prude that says: "I really don't want to do that." Then: regret, repentance, wounded pride....

We were supposed to be the Hot Feminist generation. Our role models were Beyoncé singing "Single Ladies" in a leotard and heels, and Taylor Swift celebrating female solidarity in teeny-tiny hot pants. I look forward to seeing what Millicent Fawcett wears for her new statue in Parliament Square (the Victorian Suffragist, who is to be honoured with a London statue, much to the approval of PM Theresa May).

Couldn't one school PSHE [Personal Social Health Education] lesson a term be given over to teaching girls to say: "No, I'm not OK with that." "No, I'm not ready to do that." And: "No, what sort of girl do you think I am?" This isn't a plea for convent schools and no sex before marriage. Teenage crushes, first love, romance, lust, intimacy, heartbreak: I'm cool with all of that. But not having to say yes to everything – telly rape, nudie selfies, letting him do what he wants because to say no would make you a prude.

I say: button up your cardigans, girls. Resist the tyranny of "sexy". Don't let anyone (in the bedroom or out of it) leave you ashamed or embarrassed. Enough porn chic. Time for the revolt of the prudes.'

Yes, Laura. Stand up for what you believe in: don't be bullied, and that's a feminist affirmation for sure.

Transgender issues

Feminism has never had an entirely easy relationship with the transgender issue, even though it may be said that feminism was the pathfinder and the trailblazer for transgender liberation.

I was an executive on the *London Evening Standard* in 1972 when it came to light that the much-esteemed writer and journalist James Morris had transgendered from male to female and had become Jan Morris. I had been away on leave and my deputy left me a note on return: 'The biggest sensation of the year! James Morris has become a woman!' Morris seemed an unlikely candidate to those of us who may have thought in stereotypes: adventurous, daring, having a grasp of military detail, the journalist who first reported the conquest of Mount Everest. And a married man who had fathered five children.

Sitting in El Vino discussing the sensation, some colleagues thought there was an element of the 'parodic' about trans men-to-women. They overdid the gestures of being female. They flirted in a way they believed to be feminine, with much eyelash fluttering: meanwhile, their five o'clock shave seemed to be due. The beautiful April Ashley was, then, the best-known transgender person, and she was indeed super-female and super-glamorous, but, t'was said, her hands remained those of a male.

There was some medical speculation about how a constructed vagina might function. A reporter with some medical experience suggested that nature would constantly try to knit up the artificial aperture.

Germaine Greer soon afterwards wrote a robust commentary piece for the *Standard* challenging the notion that a man could become a woman. If you're born with XY male chromosomes, no matter how much surgery you have, or how many hormone pills you take, your chromosomes remain XY. A transgender man was a man who had surgery to alter his status, but he was not a woman.

Many years later, Dr Greer held, broadly, to this position. If people wish to have a sex-change operation, they were free to do so, and free to live as the gender that they chose; but she took a different view of sexual identity. Boycotts against her speaking appearances followed. When the radio journalist Dame Jenni Murray (as did the Nigerian novelist and feminist Chimamanda Ngozi Adichie) said that men who transgendered to women were not 'real' women, since they had not grown through the experiences of being a woman – from menstruation onwards – Dame Jenni, too, was met with protests. Julie Bindel, a prominent London lawyer and gay feminist, has also registered her dissent on the transgender question: she does not accept a transgendered man as a woman. 'Those born male who are dosed with female hormones and undergo cosmetic surgery in order to present as female will never be women,' she has written.

Less has been said about women who transgender to men, but it's clear that the subject doesn't always sit comfortably with feminism. And here's one reason: possibly unfair competition. This is amply illustrated by the case of Caster

Semenya (born 1991), an astonishing South African athlete who took all before her in any race she won.

Caster came from a small village in the Limpopo region of South Aftica where she was accepted as a girl all her life, although she was always quite masculine-looking. But after Caster won the 2009 World Championships in Berlin, and having set a new national record, questions were asked about her female-ness – these questions being most repeatedly and emphatically asked by other female atheletes who felt that Caster's masculine traits gave her unfair advantage. Testosterone, the male hormone, would make a person a stronger athlete. The Italian runner, Elisa Cusma, said, 'For me, she is not a woman. She is a man. These kind of people should not run with us.'

When Ariel Levy interviewed her for *The New Yorker*, she found Caster 'breathtakingly butch', and she was duly subjected to 'gender testing' by the International Association of Athletics Federation (IAAF). Caster herself seemed bewildered, and indeed hurt by these investigations: she had always been accepted in her village for the person she was, which perhaps shows that a remote African village, where family and personality count more than scientific measurements, can be perfectly tolerant of individuals who are an intrinsic part of family and community.

But competitive athletics raises the stakes, and investigations (not all the findings were made officially public, but they were leaked) showed that Caster had three times the level of testosterone of an average female: she had been born with undescended testes instead of ovaries, and without a womb or ovaries. She was described by some as a hermaphrodite. The medical investigations were greeted with outrage in South Africa, and anger that this brilliant athlete had been subjected to humiliating tests that invaded her privacy. Caster had never, previously, been examined by a doctor, let alone a gynaecologist.

There was widespread sympathy for Caster, and the universal, liberal view was that if she thought of herself as a female, she was a female. But, in terms of biology, are you the sex (or gender) that you believe yourself to be? The transgender answer is yes – but enough women, particularly in competitive sport, still feel that a self-identified female with male levels of testosterone is unfair competition.

A medical geneticist, Eric Vilain, was quoted as saying that if you can self-define your gender, then 'anyone declaring a female gender can compete as a woman. We're moving towards one big competition, and the very predictable result is that there will be no more women winners.' There's the nub, indeed. (Later, by the way, Caster Semenya found personal happiness when she married her girlfriend.)

But in sports, as in other arenas, the issue of gender identity cannot be said to have settled. Some women clearly feel that the experience of being a woman is being 'appropriated' by people who are not, in their eyes, 'real' women.

I personally believe that in a free society, individuals can identify with whoever and whatever they like, and gender ambiguity doesn't bother me. I have met transgendered people whose personal witness is persuasive about their need to have had gender reassignment surgery. Yet can we discount biological facts? Chromosomes define sex identity, though maybe this is where the difference between 'sex' and 'gender' might be handy. 'Sex' is a biological condition; 'gender' is a social construct. Your chromosomes are your sex, but you may not identify with the biological sex of your birth.

Many feminists are supportive of transgender choice, under the general heading of LGBT (Lesbian, Gay, Bisexual and Transgender) rights. But some still dissent.

The battle of bathrooms isn't over, either, particularly among women. A headmaster in a London school told me that when one of his teaching assistants announced he was transgendering to a woman, the female teachers rose up as one and said: 'I'm not sharing the women's loos with a bloke.' Many women also do not like sharing hospital wards with those they do not identify as female, and they too have a right to affirm their preferences, and not to be boycotted, shamed or 'no-platformed'.

Transgender pronoun rules

Ever since I was made aware that folks from the city on the River Foyle favoured different names for their hometown ('Do you come from Derry?' 'Yes, I come from Londonderry'. Oh, whatever!), I have believed that people should be called whatever the heck they want to be called. So I have no problem with the transgender (or 'intersex') pronoun 'ze' replacing 'he' and 'she'.

You want me to refer to you as 'ze'? 'Ze' it is, then. It's the Derry/Londonderry rule of politesse.

Justin Trudeau's Canada has even passed a law about personal pronouns. The amendment to the Human Rights Act (Bill C-16) prohibits 'gender identity and expression', thus enforcing the use of 'ze' (also 'zi') where transgender people demand it. Woe betide anyone who adheres to Freud's principle that 'anatomy is destiny', or, worse, that biology determines gender or sex.

Sex and gender, according to progressive thinking now, are social constructs. You do not derive your gender identity from your body, or your chromosomes: it's society that has made us think in terms of gender stereotypes. We can choose our gender identity.

Dissent from this view – especially in Canada – at your peril. Professor Jordan Peterson, psychology professor at the University of Toronto, has called the new pronoun laws 'compelled speech': those who refuse to comply may be brought before the courts for 'hate speech'. Professor Peterson was instructed that he must comply.

It may be good manners to use 'ze' and 'zi' on request. But there's a difference, surely, between courtesy and the State enforcing what you choose to say?

The triumph of transgender ideology is now unstoppable. In Britain (where there's been a ten-fold increase in demand for referrals to gender identity clinics) the education authorities have been pressing forward with teaching young children about transgenderism. The National Union of Teachers has recommended that children as young as four should be taught positive transgender values – to combat 'hate speech' against people who change sex or people who reject the 'binary' concept of sexuality. Top London schools like St Paul's have introduced 'gender-neutral' protocols to allow pupils to choose whatever gender identity they wish.

The British academic, Dr Joanna Williams from Canterbury, caused a furore at an education conference by saying that teaching transgender policies would confuse young children: they don't need to be taught about 'gender fluidity' in primary school, and since the transgender issue only affects about 1 per cent of the population, it's a 'waste of time and money' to dedicate educational policies to it.

Dr Williams's common sense is against the grain of current fashion. Transgender policies (and politics) are gaining ground everywhere, and those who object may be accused of fomenting hate speech, or anti-trans bigotry.

Where does this ideology come from? The philosophical source of gender theory is Judith Butler, whose complex and sometimes difficult academic works on gender theory have attained global status. Professor Butler objects to words like 'masculine' and 'feminine', since they represent an unacceptable 'norm', and 'norms' are imposed on us by social practice and patriarchal institutions.

All gender stereotypes must be challenged. All sexual identity stereotypes must be challenged. (And sexual identity does not necessarily correlate with sexual orientation.)

Although gender theory affirms that we are all on a spectrum between 'masculine' and 'feminine', Professor Butler nonetheless deplores the words 'masculine' and 'feminine'. Calling some women 'masculine' and some men 'feminine' is itself a violence against gay, transgender and intersex people. It is these 'norms' that have led to violence and hate crimes against all LGBTQI (lesbian, gay, bi-sexual, transgender, queer and intersex) people.

Actually, I can buy the idea of gender fluidity. Some women are more masculine (if you'll forgive the word) and some men more feminine (ditto), and it's interesting to observe that. I shop like a man: dash into the shop, quick decision, dash out again. A professor of mathematics once analysed the way I write, and concluded that I must be a man in disguise, because my sentence structures are masculine. If you say so, prof!

And anyway, the sexes do tend to merge much more with age. Older women become 'virilised', in the medical term (more like men), and men grow feminine with age, soft-skinned and rosy-cheeked.

However, this is straying into the area that is rejected and rebuffed by gender theory – that gender is based on biology and chromosomes. As already mentioned, Germaine Greer was silenced ('no-platformed') in British academia for saying she did not accept that a male could become a female by the process of surgery and hormone treatment. The biological interpretation of sex/gender is simply not acceptable in respectable circles anymore.

It was Victor Hugo, I think, who said that there is nothing as powerful as an idea whose time has come. And now is the time for gender theory.

Canada certainly is in the forefront of gender theory and transgender rights. Recently an eight-month-old Canadian baby was the first ever to be officially registered as 'gender unknown'. The infant, child of a 'non-binary trans person', Kori Doty, will choose its own gender when it (or 'ze') has 'the sense of self and command of vocabulary to do so.'

And anyone who gives it a pink or blue toy, or otherwise strays into the explosive field of what little boys or little girls are made of, will surely fall foul of Mr Trudeau's transgender protection laws.

Ursuline Order

The Ursuline Order of nuns is the world's oldest teaching order of religious sisters, and a pioneering influence in the field of women's education. It was founded by St Angela of Merici, a very remarkable Italian woman who was born at Desenzano, on the shores of Lake Garda, in 1474. Like many enterprising historical individuals, she was left an orphan at an early age – though her family had been merchants so she seems to have had some means. She began teaching catechisms to local children, and she was asked to do similar work in other parts of Italy. She travelled up and down Italy on horseback before going off to the Holy Land and Rome on pilgrimages. In 1535, when Angela was sixty-one, she, along with a number of younger companions and followers, dedicated themselves to God and to the education of girls. Angela's approach was what we would now call 'child-centered': this company of women, uncloistered, and following a flexible regime, often taught children and young girls in their own home.

The enlightened attitudes of the Ursuline nuns (named after St Ursula, a fifth-century German martyr) spread its influence down the centuries: my mother attended an Ursuline convent in Co. Sligo in 1920 and never forgot the open and encouraging attitudes of her Ursuline teacher, Mother Scholastica. At a time when the name of Oscar

Wilde wasn't mentioned in polite circles – his conviction was considered so shameful that it was virtually taboo – Mother was dared by her fellows in class to ask the nun: 'Why was Oscar Wilde sent to jail?'

Mother Scholastica turned from the blackboard, and said, very coolly, 'Oh, just for loving another man', and, unperturbed, continued with the lesson.

The education of women became one of the first causes in the advancement of Victorian feminism; the pioneering Emily Davies, Frances Mary Buss and Dorothea Beale were terrific figures in the education of girls, more than three centuries after the Ursuline order was established. Access to education was really the first feminist frontier, and 'Miss Beale and Miss Buss' were crusading reformers who opened the doors in the modern period. Rather mockingly, they were stereotyped as spinster schoolmarms with the doggerel: 'Miss Buss and Miss Beale/Cupid's darts do not feel/How different from us/Miss Beal and Miss Buss.' Like many a religious sister before them, they set aside much of their personal lives to bring women's education forward.

Unconscious bias

For some time, feminists have been aware of – and wary of – 'unconscious bias' in, for example, a job interview, where the employer's prejudice is unconsciously lurking against, or in favour of, a particular candidate. It can be exercised according to gender, or class, or age, or race, or religion.

There are interesting examples of where it has been exercised positively, if quite disastrously: British intelligence allowed a raft of pro-Soviet spies to thrive in their ranks because there was unconscious bias in favour of the old-school tie. It's unlikely that Burgess, Philby and MacClean could have been free to go on working for Stalin and Co. if they hadn't been at Cambridge together, and jolly well part of the establishment in the first place.

Unconscious bias is bad for business – if, say, you're hiring someone just because they are in the same Freemason's Lodge with you – and it's also unfair and unjust. Everyone should, as the nuns in our school used to say, 'examine their conscience' as to whether this is occurring, and then correct it. We should form judgements on evidence, not fancies or stereotypes.

The trouble is with the human brain, which makes instant judgements. I sometimes complain that complete strangers patronise me as a ditzy old dear – 'Hello, darling, are you all right there?' – while respectfully addressing a tall young man in his twenties with 'Good afternoon, sir.' Tallness, maleness and sometimes commanding youth are instantly registered in that part of the brain which jumps to conclusions as a superior specimen, whereas short, plump, old grannies must be powerless little dears who are not of much account.

One can rail against this, or take it as an opportunity to practice humility, as T. S. Eliot counsels us to do.

However, a friend of mine of the same vintage, who wears stylish designer clothes, says that she never meets with this attitude: she's always treated with respect, even deference. That's perhaps because the brain clocks that a woman in exquisitely styled clothes is probably upper caste. Money and class must always be factored into all social analysis. This matters more in some situations than in others: it is of little account when at the check-out at Marks & Spencer, but it can be vital when jobs, promotions, education, and financial positions are at stake.

Vaginas

Eve Ensler's play *The Vagina Monologues* has been trans-lated into around fifty languages and performed in over 140 countries since its first performance in New York City in 1998. It has attracted truly stellar participants, includ-ing Cate Blanchett, Kate Winslet, Gillian Anderson, Melanie Griffith, Meera Syal, Joel Richardson, Ruby Wax, Jane Lapotaire and support from Whoopi Goldberg, Susan Sarandon, Glenn Close, Winona Ryder, Lily Tomlin, Calista Flockhart and Gloria Steinem. It is a collection of reflections on the female vagina and its contextual parts, and has evidently prompted many women to think about this part of their body, and to be open and candid about the functions of sexual pleasure.

It has encouraged women in their thousands to chant 'vagina' in unison (as well as 'vulva', 'clitoris' and 'labia') as an exercise in self-liberation from the prudish and repressive mores of yesteryear, where they might have been referred to as 'private parts' only. Although in the interests of balance, it should be said that there are some – entirely modern – individuals who prefer to regard their 'private parts' as just that: private. There are even some individuals for whom the veiled and the allusive is more erotic than the open and the candid, but as my dear mother used to say, '*chacun à son goût*'.

Funds raised by the performance of *The Vagina Monologues* have gone to support shelters for abused women and campaigns to halt violence against women. Whether shouting 'cunt' and 'vagina' in a chorus has succeeded in reducing violence against women we do not know: we still await the research.

The Vagina Monologues explores many experiences and sensations around this very significant part of the female anatomy, yet it takes Eve Ensler two years to consider one of the most obvious experiences of all. 'I had been performing this piece for over two years when it suddenly occurred to me that there were no pieces about birth,' she wrote in the published text. 'It was a bizarre omission. Although when I told a journalist this recently, he asked me: "What's the connection?"'

For some, evidently, sex education does not include the information that, except in cases of surgical caesarean section, the vagina is the birth passage that allows a baby to exit the womb.

Ms Ensler goes on to explain how this aspect of the vagina eventually came to her (writing in 2001):

'Almost twenty-one years ago I adopted a son, Dylan... Last year he and his wife, Shiva, had a baby. They asked me to be present for the birth. I don't think, in all my investigation, that I really understood vaginas until this moment. If I was in awe of them before the birth of my granddaughter, Colette, I am certainly in deep worship now.'

And there follows an elegiac monologue-poem about the miracle of the vagina as an agency and usher of new life, in conception and in delivery. And so it is.

Violence against women

In a primitive situation – supposing we were casting our imaginations back to cave-man times – it is evident that males were physically bigger and stronger than females, so when men have threatened (or carried out) violence against women, perhaps it was because they could. The restrictions of civilisation have sought to restrain these reflexes, as have the bonds of affection, the protection of families – Michael Caine, the film star, has recalled that in his East-End childhood, a fellow treated a girl well because otherwise her brothers would come around and give him a right hiding. As society developed, the law sought to deter and restrain such violence.

Under the rule of law, an assault of any kind is a breach of the law. Rightly so. It is to the credit of the feminist movement that violence, including domestic abuse, against women has become a focus for the police and the law.

Yet here's an odd thing: violence against women tends to be proportionately higher in developed and sophisticated societies, and proportionately lower in less developed and less advanced cultures.

Consider the homicide statistics by gender, as issued by the United Nationals Office on Drugs and Crime. (Worldwide, 78.7 per cent of homicide victims are male, which means that just over 21 per cent are female. 96 per cent of the perpetrators are men.) Here are the statistics for the percentage of female victims in less developed societies:

Afghanistan: 13 per cent
Anguilla: 0 per cent
Central African Republic: 14.4 per cent
Colombia: 8.4 per cent
Guatemala: 11.1 per cent
Malawi: 12.5 per cent
Nepal: 2.2 per cent
Paraguay 11.2 per cent
Trinidad and Tobago: 8.3 per cent
Uganda: 13.8 per cent

Now compare these figures with developed – and much richer – countries:

Austria: 40.2 per cent
Czech Republic: 45.7 per cent
Denmark: 34 per cent
Finland: 46.1 per cent
France: 37.9 per cent
Iceland:100 per cent*
Italy: 30 per cent
Korea: 52.5 per cent
Romania: 37.5 per cent
Slovenia: 42.9 per cent
Switzerland: 50 per cent.

*This figure is skewed because in the year under review (2010), there was only one homicide committed – and the victim was female.

Percentages don't reflect the actual numbers of course: South Africa has a very high homicide rate (16, 259 victims), with 15.4 per cent of victims being women; Austria only had seventy-seven homicides, of which 40 per cent were female. The proportion of women murdered in Finland is getting on for half – but the total number of homicides was only eighty-nine (as against Argentina's 2,237 annual toll, of which only 16 per cent were female.)

We may draw the conclusion, however, that when a society is generally more violent, it is men who are more likely to be the victims of violence. When a society is more law-abiding, the proportion of female victims increases. This indicates that domestic violence is probably the most intractable, because it is the most difficult to police: more law and order forces cannot account for everything that goes on behind closed doors.

Alcohol abuse can, clearly, aggravate domestic violence, though Margaret Martin, the experienced director of Women's Aid in Ireland, notes that alcohol is sometimes the excuse, not the reason. In one survey, 27 per cent of respondents said that alcohol was 'always' involved while 29 per cent said it was 'never' a factor. (For the rest, it was 'sometimes'.)

Domestic violence should be reported and prosecuted wherever and whenever, but there is a question mark all the same: how much can the State control private life? And how much would we want it to monitor our private lives? This is a dilemma: in the age of the internet, many of us feel that there is already rather more surveillance on private life than we might always want.

Legislation against domestic violence and abuse has recently tended to include 'emotional abuse' alongside physical abuse – this is the case in Britain, where Theresa May is a keen campaigner against domestic abuse (as is Camilla, Duchess of Cornwall). In Ireland, Sharon O'Halloran of 'Safe Ireland' – a fine organisation supporting victims of domestic violence (they receive 50,000 calls for assistance a year) has written that 'Psychological abuse can leave the deepest wounds of all'. 'Coercive control' is now categorised as a 'serious form of abuse', and according to Ms O'Halloran, may be a prelude to physical assault.

I find this very ambivalent territory. If verbal abuse is on a par with physical violence, then women are just as likely to be the perpetrators as men.

I can think of many couples where the woman is the psychologically dominant partner, and I have seen a woman needle, manipulate and control a man. I worked with a couple a few years ago where the wife's abuse of the husband was almost unbearable to witness – constant, repeated and systematic humiliation. He sat there taking it, and even apologising. Maybe he loved her nonetheless; maybe he was a masochist and sought punishment, as some men seek out 'dominatrixes' who beat them; maybe he felt he had no other option but to stay with her; or maybe it was a case that he blamed himself.

But if verbal abuse is a crime, should I have reported this scene to the police? Alerted the social services? Suggest he seek a domestic abuse refuge? My attitude is that that adult individuals have to sort out their own couple psychology.

'Controlling' and 'coercive' behaviour happens in work situations as well as in domestic set-ups. I've experienced this– and just as much from women as from men. But when it comes to physical violence, overall, the difference between the genders is stark. Just to repeat: globally, 96 per cent of perpetrators of homicides are male, and just over 78 per cent of victims are male.

A clear indication that *la différence* still applies to the sexes. Physically, women are simply much less prone to violence.

But when it comes to words, females are perfectly capable of verbal aggressions. Included, perhaps, of that which men have called, down the centuries, 'nagging'.

Women carrying water

Before the advent of taps that ran water into the kitchen, it was often the duty of women to bring water from the well (and it still is, in some less-developed societies) and from the village pump. In Connemara, in the west of Ireland, my own cousins first got running water around about 1947; it made an almost miraculous change to the lives of the women, who before that had to carry the water from the nearby pump.

I have a friend who is now in her sixties who remembers that water had to be carried from the local source, near Claudy, Co. Derry/Londonderry, as late as the 1970s. Her mother often carried this wellwater, as did she and her sisters – she never remembers the menfolk participating in water carrying.

We should be thankful that times have changed; the status of women has changed. And we owe some gratitude, too, to the engineers who developed processes of delivering running water into our homes. When the quarterly bill arrives from the water supply company, I pay it gladly, remembering how those women, within my living memory, carried water, and that women in developing countries still do so.

Women on board

Should women be better represented on the boards of companies and corporations? The admirable Susan Morrissey (mother of nine children, as it happens) is the City of London campaigner who set up the 30% Club, advocating that boards should be at least 30 per cent female.

A very good aim, if the women in question are the right candidates. Quotas to ensure women are advanced as company directors are less dependable: that makes candidates open to the suggestion that they are 'lame ducks' who had to be assisted to their place at the table, and that's an unenviable position. I've been put in such a position myself, where I was promoted to a position for which I was mortifyingly underqualified, and I wouldn't wish the experience on anyone. But it's surely in the best interests of companies and corporations to be imaginative in finding suitable female candidates – as well as being fair to deserving male candidates.

Personally, I'd rather watch paint dry than sit on a company board.

We should give women every chance to be sufficiently well-represented in the commanding positions of business and administration. But the thought of compelled quotas isn't my idea of liberation.

X – a 'girly' sign-off?

The written symbol for a kiss has become a common sign-off on emails and text messages. My colleague Deborah Maby, journalist and editor, finds it maddening to receive this 'kiss' sign from people she hardly knows 'on emails, texts, WhatsApp, Facebook, Instagram and even Twitter. But where did it come from, this coquettish false intimacy?' Sometimes, annoyingly, there are even two such marks of 'x'.

'I don't wish to sound unsisterly, but I do think women are more complicit than men,' she wrote in *The Oldie*. 'They can't wait to start adding kisses to their communications. My partner tells me he often gets work-related messages from women he barely knows with an x are the end.' For Deborah, the practice has cheapened true intimacy.

I must confess: I do it. But then we all kiss each other a lot more these days, and quite often, people kiss me as they are introduced. Fashions change – and indeed these changes are often led by women.

Youth and age

Women complain that once over fifty (or sometimes in their forties), they feel they become 'invisible'. 'You really do become invisible when you hit middle age,' an interviewee tells Laura Bates, author of *Everyday Sexism*. Others say 'I'm now fifty-one and I definitely am beginning to feel invisible.' 'I'm forty-three and disappearing.' 'As a grandmother of three, and in my mid fiftiess, I find I am invisible everywhere!' 'I am sixty years old on Thursday but have been invisible for at least ten years. Older people, women especially, just live on the sidelines of society. That's how it feels, anyway.'

I am not, personally, bothered about being in the age-bracket of invisibilty: I rather like it. It's satisfying sitting on the terrace of a nice café – my mother's choice of location was the Café de la Paix, near Opéra, in Paris – and just people-watching, and people-listening too. Gratifyingly, nobody takes the slightest notice of an old biddy in a corner watching the world. That's an enormous advantage to this 'invisibility'.

To each season in life there are gifts, and to each season there are compensations. People can be very nice to young girls just because they are young and beautiful – all young people seem to me to have a striking, luminous beauty. I wasn't beautiful when I was young, but many people were kind and indulgent and encouraging to me because I was young and eager and ambitious (and ditzy). And for all that we whinged about 'patriarchy', many men were extraordinarily kind and encouraging to me – and to other young women of my generation – in our careers. Youth is a gift! Appreciate it! Make the best of it! Build happy memories! Don't look back and think that youth is wasted on the young.

Zita and the women saints

'Herstory' is a worthy attempt to recapture for 'history' the feminist (or even feminine) aspects of the past that have so often been invisible or omitted. Where are the women's voices in history (herstory)? Perhaps secularists have sometimes forgotten to look in the standard *Dictionary of Saints*, in which women abound. These women are characters in history, they are not mystical or supernatural phenomena: they lived real lives and here is the last entry in the biography of the saints – St Zita.

Zita was a humble domestic servant, born in Lucca, Italy in 1218. She became a household maid at the age of twelve, working for a wealthy weaver's family, and remained a serving maid all her life. Her exemplary character and care for the poor won her much respect and at her death, at the age of fifty, she was popularly regarded as a local saint and a patroness of maid-servants. She was canonised in 1748, and her emblem is a bunch of keys.

This is an obscure young woman whose life was of modest status, but made enough impact on her community to be regarded as a saint, and 500 years later, to be canonised.

The prominent women of history are often ladies of high rank, but female saints come from all walks of life. The simple peasant girl features as frequently as the queen or aristocrat: St Germaine (d. 1601) was not only a simple shepherdess, but probably a simpleton. She was also 'unhealthy, scrofulous, and with a withered hand'. She was cruelly treated, being a stepchild, and slept in a cupboard under the stairs. People were unkind to her, but Germaine had a good character and never responded in an ugly way. One day her stepmother accused her of stealing bread: Germaine opened her apron and it was full of spring flowers. She died young and from about 1644, her grave became a place of pilgrimage and miracles were ascribed to her.

Some of these holy women were powerful, like St Hilda, Abbess of Northumbria, who commanded a double monastery of men and women (St Hilda's College in Cambridge is named after her). Some became legends, like St Hildegarde of the Rhine (d. 1179): music composer, essayist on the natural sciences, and all-round wise woman who corresponded with four popes, two emperors and Henry II of England. St Bathild (d. 680) was an Englishwoman who married King Clovis II of France (having been first captured by pirates) and after his death, became queen regent. She was an early campaigner against the slave trade.

The life of Bridget of Sweden (d. 1373) is a significant illustration of the power and influence that women of rank could achieve in the middle ages. Married to a nobleman, they had eight children (including a daughter, Saint Catherine of Vadstena). Bridget was a commanding chatelaine and took to advising the king, Magnus III. Upon being widowed, she travelled to Rome and took to advising the Pope. She travelled on pilgrimages to Rome, the Holy Land and Santiago di Compostela. She launched an order of nuns in Rome, the Brigettines, who were responsible for looking after the poor and sick, and her funeral attracted an immense crowd.

Some of these women led unusual lives, like St Marina (for whom we have no dates), known as a woman monk – she grew up disguised as a boy, and was accused of fathering a child, but found innocent and exonerated; some could be folkloric rather than documented, and yet have attracted some interest and veneration, like the Irish St Dympna (also date unknown), said to have been the daughter of a pagan prince who, alas, seems to have been a sexual abuser – or a would-be abuser, anyway. She fled to Antwerp with her chaplain; the abusive father pursued and killed her. After her death she became the patron saint of mental disorders, and was said through her intercession to cure depression and epilepsy. If Dympna is a folklore legend, she nonetheless attracted a cult following, as did her fellow-countrywoman, St Attracta (6th century), who set up a hospice and a shelter for travellers by Lough Gara (around the area now called Killaraght).

Joan of Arc rightly retains her heroic and emblematic status – an uneducated teenage girl who led the King of France into battle. But saints were also peacemakers: Brigid of Ireland broke her father's sword in a rebuttal of war.

Maria Goretti died as a victim of rape, and surely earns her place in the canon. Jane of Chantal was a widow who walked out on her children – she stepped over the prostrate body of her teenage son – to found a religious order. She inspired St Vincent de Paul, and the son who pleaded with her not to leave home became the father of the writer Madame de Sevigné.

Women as saints is a field that awaits greater attention, research and exploration than it has as yet received in feminist history, for it is here that many of the lost voices of women's lives – at every rank – may be found.

Epilogue

Am I a feminist? Are you?

Looking back to my youth, I think feminism was, for me, a route to knowledge and a way of making sense of life as a woman. It was also, of course, exciting and radical, and in tune with the times that were a-changing, Dylan-like. But, because I left school at sixteen, went straight into a working life – you didn't get to go to university in Ireland in the 1960s unless you were either clever enough to do so, or well-off enough to lark around for three years with chaps in sports cars (how the less privileged saw it) – my education was unfinished. Reading women like Germaine Greer, Kate Millett (Sexual Politics) and Eva Figes (Patriarchal Attitudes) made a big impact on me: these women knew their stuff!

Most of the feminists I came to know had also been greatly influenced by Betty Friedan's The Feminine Mystique, and the part that I most vividly recall was the passage about a housewife going about her daily routine chores, and asking herself: 'Is this all there is?'

Perhaps the pursuit of feminism was my own, self-devised university-of-life course in 'women's studies'. Life as a learning process.

Feminism has been a social movement of huge importance over the past fifty years, changing women's (and men's) lives, and yet it is sometimes ambivalently viewed by women. Polls and studies often indicate that women themselves don't always like being labelled as 'feminists' – it can still seem 'strident' and sometimes even 'looney fringe'.

Yet women benefit from many of the reforms that feminism has wrought, or has prompted. As Joanna Williams points out in her book Women versus Feminism, feminism is part of a whole raft of social and technological change, and in the fifty years since we moved from the typewriter to the laptop computer and mobile-phone-that-does-everything, there has been a lot thrown into the mix.

There are also many factions within feminism: there are 'equity feminists', who believe in equality before the law and in the workplace. There are feminists who believe that men and women are the same, and there are feminists who believe that men and women are different. There are 'Amazon feminists', as Camille Paglia calls herself; her construct was to be a warrior, be brave, and above all, be opposed to those 'victim feminists', who see women as always the victim of patriarchy, or the law, or society. Increasingly, there are 'gender feminists', whose guru is Judith Butler, who see gender itself as a 'social construct' – it is society that defines us, not biology.

There are Marxist feminists, and there are many socialist feminists – de Beauvoir herself believed you must be a socialist to be a feminist. But actually, there are Conservative feminists too – the leader of the Scottish Conservative Party, Ruth Davidson, has proved herself to be a sunny and effective example of the type. There are post-feminists, libertarian feminists, evolutionary feminists, even biological-determinist feminists – those radicals who claim that men and women are biologically different, and this will influence their choices and decisions. There are commercial feminists – they have observed that the feminist product sells – and fashionista feminists – those who stride the catwalk wearing a 'feminist' skimpy T-shirt that costs $500 (made in Bangladesh for pennies). And there are quite a few let's-jump-on-the-bandwagon feminists of both sexes. It amuses me to see individuals who once argued against equal pay (on the trade- union principle that men had to earn a 'family wage') now advance themselves as the most stalwart of feminists.

Many people pick and choose, and that's not meant to be disparaging: it impresses me that the most surprising women – otherwise, sometimes, conventional – will come out with a feminist reflex, from memory, that they really feel strongly about. 'And do you know, I found out later, I was doing exactly the same job as he was – but I was being paid 30 per cent less? Outrageous!' Or 'When I think that I had to get a man to counter-sign my application for a mortgage, when the man in question was hopeless with money!' Or 'I had to show an engagement ring at the family planning clinic before they'd prescribe me the pill! What business was it of theirs whether I was married or not?' Others will look back on their mother's experience and think how unfair life was for her.

You might not accept the whole package marked 'feminism', but within broader feminism, there is usually something for everyone. Nearly everyone finds some issue they feel is right and just, even if they don't identify themselves as full-on feminists.

Feminism is not a tightly-organised society like the Freemasons, or a club where you must obey the rules to get elected. It's a broad social and political movement, and, therefore, anyone is entitled to define their own feminism. I do see myself, therefore, as my own, self-defined feminist: a sort of eclectic emancipationist, tested by experience. Why not pick and choose the bits that seem workable and leave aside those elements that don't?

Pick and mix is fine, but there are contradictions within broad feminist thinking that need clarifying. There is a tension between 'choice' and 'equality', for example (just as there can be a conflict between 'inclusion' and 'diversity' – it's a lot harder to include everyone when they are all very different).

If you suggest that everyone is entitled to choose their lifestyle, people will undoubtedly choose differently.

True equality can only exist (as Margaret Thatcher concluded from her reading of Hayek) at quite a simple, tribal, social level. As soon as there is development, there is difference. Then again, less developed societies aren't particularly favourable to women. In Communist Albania – which became a less developed society under Enver Hoxha – I saw women doing backbreaking work in the fields while men sat under the olive trees.

I support equity feminism but I also find 'equality' complicated because it seems to me there are situations in which women should be favoured. 'Women and children first' was a good point of courtesy precisely because, in the raw state of survival, it was often 'women and children last'. I notice this in airport security queues, as big, sturdy men hustle ahead of me – because they can. 'Ladies first' is a nice fiction, because otherwise ladies may well be last. More seriously, when Richard, my husband, was reporting on the Biafran war, he was distressed to observe that fit young men were always the first to be fed, and women and children had little priority. 'Warriors first,' was the principle.

In our societies, I believe that one situation in which women should be favoured, rather than simply be equal, is motherhood. When it was suggested in Ireland that men and women should have equal parenting leave, rather than mothers having more time off than fathers, Leo Varadkar (now Taoiseach) made the observation that mothers need to recover, physically, from childbirth, and it's a good idea if they also breastfeed. Men don't need such a period of physical recovery. (As a medical doctor, he had clocked this.)

This also brings up the forbidden 'N' word – 'Nature'. I find Camille Paglia's reasoning powerful because she has so thoroughly examined the role that nature exercises in all our lives. And if you don't take account of nature you can disadvantage women: consider the layout of men's and women's toilets to which I have alluded in this text. Lavatories should not have 'equal' space: women need more toilets and more sophisticated toilets, too. Every building should have twice the toilet capacity for women as for men. This is both a basic reality and a metaphor of difference.

If nature had no part in the shaping of our capabilities, then men and women would play the same games, compete together in athletics and kick footballs against one another. (As that accidental feminist, Princess Anne, has said: 'where men and women compete against each other, it usually involves a horse'.)

This isn't to say we passively 'accept' nature – manners and morals developed to overcome it. But we may be delusional if we ignore it.

Biology matters. It's not just a 'social construct'.

In many areas, feminism has been progressive and enlightening, even if, in some cases, it has also been daft and shrill. Not everyone wants to join the 'Pussy Riots', wearing a knitted hat designed to invoke a vagina (but if that's what floats your boat, go for it). On the abortion issue, it's understandable that mainstream feminism has taken a hard line that it's a woman choice – 'without apology or charge' – since this is a logical step in exercising total birth control. Contraception can fail and women can become unwillingly pregnant. (Whether we ever have 'total control' of anything is another question.)

Polls show that where abortion is legal, the public has little appetite for making it illegal. But polls also show that the public at large, including women, have 'mixed feelings' about approving abortion, and have quite a strong dislike of late abortion, except in a serious medical emergency. Only 1 per cent of the British public would support a woman's right to choose abortion right up to birth – although some radical doctors have voted to introduce this protocol. There is a recognition among the general public, and more emphatically among women, that the unborn/foetus acquires rights and deserves some protection.

There isn't going to be agreement on the abortion debate, and where there is a political battle being fought – as in Ireland – feelings will be highly sensitised and discourse adversarial. But there has to be room for respecting conscience and ethics – and facing medical facts too. The developments in embryology and fetology will soon make it seem obscurantist, even scientifically backward, not to face the facts that are occurring in this field. Artificial wombs, ectogenesis, foetal transplants, highly sophisticated methods of surrogacy – all these developments are on the horizon. 'Artificial wombs, able to gestate a foetus outside the body, will completely upend feminism's arguments on bodily autonomy,' wrote Eleanor Robertson in The Guardian.

And there's something else that is worth saying: this is an extraordinarily profound subject – the very nub of Hamlet's question – 'To be or not to be'. Woman has been worshipped for being at the heart of the creation of life, and for being that heart itself. Ann Furedi, the director of Britain's largest abortion provider, has acknowledged a sense of 'the miracle of life', even in dealing with terminating pregnancies. A feminist should be allowed to honour that 'miracle of life' as she has thought it through for herself. A feminist should be allowed to reflect on the miracle, and the honour, of bearing life. And perhaps a feminist philosopher should, rather than disparage conception, affirm ownership of its significance.

But think it through for yourself. I believe the most vital aspect of being a feminist is just this: think for yourself. Be independent. Show solidarity with those you support, but don't comply with 'groupthink'. Make up your own mind. Reflect on your experiences. Affirm intellectual autonomy. Listen to others, but don't be defined by others and their values. Come to your own conclusions, and stand up for yourself.

Feminism has been a learning tool for me, but it has also led me on to other, wider fields of enquiry, and revealed to me the richness of history and the significance of context. It is gratifying to see younger generations of women having the freedom to achieve fulfilment and contributing so much to the public sphere. Feminism opened the door to a wider world – a world where I wouldn't want feminist values alone to form a kind of gender sectarianism. May it also do for you.

Mary Kenny, July 2017

Select bibliography

Adichie, Chimamanda Ngozi. *We Should All Be Feminists.* Fourth Estate, 2014.

Bates, Laura. *Everyday Sexism.* Simon & Schuster, 2015.

Brittain, Vera. *Lady into Woman: a history of women from Victoria to Elizabeth II.* A. Dakers, 1953.

Butler, Elizabeth. *Battle Artist.* First published 1922. Fisher paperback, 1993.

Butler, Judith. *Undoing Gender.* Psychology Press, 2004.

Crispin, Jessa. *Why I am Not a Feminist: A feminist manifesto.* Melville House, 2017.

De Beauvoir, Simone. *The Second Sex.* Gallimard, 1949. Vintage, 1997.

De Riencourt, Amaury de. *Woman and Power in History.* Honeyglen, 1974.

Ensler, Eve. *The Vagina Monologues.* Virago, 2001.

Friedan, Betty. *The Feminine Mystique.* Gollancz, 1963.

Furedi, Ann. *The Moral Case for Abortion.* Palgrave Macmillan, 2016.

Gordon, Felicia. *The Integral Feminist: Madeleine Pelletier 1874-1939 – Feminism, Socialism and Medicine.* Polity Press, 1990.

Greer, Germaine. *The Female Eunuch.* MacGibbon & Kee, 1970.

— *The Change: Women, Ageing and the Menopause.* Penguin, 1992.

Gruenbaum, Ellen. T*he Female Circumcision Controversy – an anthropological perspective.* University of Pennsylvania Press, 2001.

Harding, Esther. *Women's Mysteries, Ancient and Modern.* First published 1955. HarperCollins, 1976.

Holtby, Winifred. *Women and a Changing Civilisation.* John Lane, 1934.

Kenyatta, Jomo. *Facing Mount Kenya: The Tribal Life of the Gikuyu.* Vintage Books/Random House, 1965.

Kitzinger, Sheila. *Women as Mothers.* Random House, 1978.

Kamm, Josephine. *How Different From Us: A Biography of Miss Buss and Miss Beale.* Bodley Head, 1958.

Hufton, Olwen. *The Prospect Before Her: A History of Women in Western Europe.* Fontana, 1997.

Levy, Ariel. *The Rules do not Apply.* Fleet/Random House, 2017.

Llewelyn Davies, Margaret (ed). *Life as we have known it – co-operative working women.* Co-Op Guild, 1931. (Forward by Virginia Woolf).

Morgan, Robin (ed). *Sisterhood is Powerful: an anthology of writing from the women's liberation movement.* Random House, 1970.

Paglia, Camille. *Sex, Art and American Culture.* Viking, 1992.

— *Free Women, Free Men: Sex, Gender and Feminism.* Pantheon Books, 2017.

Pinker, Steven. *The Blank Slate: The Modern Denial of Human Nature.* Penguin, 2003.

Phillips, Angela. *The Trouble With Boys.* Pandora, 1994.

Potts, Diggory & Peel. *Abortion.* Cambridge University Press, 1977.

Sandberg, Sheryl. *Lean In: Women, Work and the Will to Lead.* W.H. Allen, London 2013.

Sinclair, Andrew. *Prohibition: The Era of Excess.* Faber, 1962.

Shaw, Bernard. *Mrs Warren's Profession*. Broadview Editions, 2005.

Smith, Harold (ed). *British Feminism in the 20th Century*. Edward Elgar, 1990.

Spencer, Samia (ed). *Frenchwomen and the Age of Enlightenment*. University of Indiana Press, 1984.

Stopper, Anne. *Monday at Gaj's: The Story of the Irish Women's Liberation Movement*. Liffey Press, 2006.

Strachey, Ray. *The Cause: A Short History of the Women's Movement in Great Britain*. First published 1928. Reprinted Virago, 1978.

Uglow, Jennifer (ed). *The Macmillan Dictionary of Women's Biography*. Macmillan, 1982.

Vinogradova, Lyuba. *Avenging Angels: Soviet Women Snipers on the Eastern Front*. Maclehose Press, Quercus, 2017.

Walter, Natasha. *Living Dolls: The Return of Sexism*. Little, Brown, 2011.

Walsh, Michael (ed). *Dictionary of Christian Biography*. Continuum, 2001.

West, Lindy. *Shrill – Notes from a Loud Woman*. Hachette, 2016.

Williams, Joanna. *Women vs Feminism – Why we all need liberating from the Gender Wars*. Emerald Publishing, 2017.

Wolf, Naomi. *Misconceptions: Truth, Lies and the Unexpected on the Journey to Motherhood*. Chatto & Windus, 2001.

Notes on sources

Actor/Actress: Helen McCrory was speaking to the *London Evening Standard* on 6 June 2017. Lesley Mackie and Beth Watson kindly contacted me after I asked the question of whether 'actresses' should be 'actors' in The Stage.

Beauty: Naomi Wolf's *The Beauty Myth* and Natasha Walter's *Living Dolls* posit the suggestion that the beauty business manipulates women, and is a source of inequality.

Contraception and women's health: Older doctors recalled to me their early experience of visiting Dublin as a particular centre for multiparous mothers with health problems. Several essays in Harold Smith's *British Feminism in the 20th Century* reprise the history of attitudes to contraception, which was far from respectable until the 1960s. Margaret Llewelyn Davies' *Life As We Have Known It* contains touching accounts of the struggles of mothers in the early twentieth century. Jonathan Eig's *The Birth of the Pill* chronicles much of the background information around the appearance of the contraceptive pill.

Division of labour: Mrs Pankhurst's tribute to the respect with which men in the frontier states of America treated women appears in her own autobiography.

Divorce: A vivid account of Caroline Norton's struggle to obtain a divorce in the nineteenth century, and most especially her fight for custody of her children, which at that time was always awarded to the father, appears in Ray Strachey's *The Cause*. Mary Cummins, who died in 1998, was an Irish feminist with strong radical views, but she was also a countrywoman who understood rural life, and a truthful reporter. She concluded that divorce, and family break-up, in farming life was hugely problematic – a point not always grasped by a metropolitan mind-set.

Equality: Anthony Atkinson (d. 2017) was a distinguished economist whose primary work was on the question of inequality. His best-known book is *Inequality – What Can Be Done?* Chrystia Freeland, author of *Plutocrats*, is also a very knowledgeable source on the growing global inequalities and has given TED talks on this theme. Pay rates cited are available in the public realm.

Everyday sexism and the 'wolf whistle': Miriam Gross was writing in *The Spectator* on 28 January 2017. Some police forces in Britain have taken the decision to treat 'wolf whistles' as hate crimes (*Daily Telegraph*, 14 July 2016.)

Marjorie Wallace's more light-hearted view of sexism appeared in a report in the *London Evening Standard* on 23 May 2013.

Faith and women: the Pew Research Centre has found that women as a group are nearly always more religious than men – and particularly among Christians. A particularly interesting report was carried out on 22 March 2016 which found that the 'gender gap' in faith was virtually universal and is available on their website. The *Times of London* reported on 19 June 2017 that more women were becoming bishops, and training for ordination in the Anglican faith.

Fear of feminism: Professor Dennis Hayes was quoted in the *Daily Telegraph* on 29 June 2017.

French women in the eighteenth century and thereafter: See Samia I. Spencer's *Frenchwomen and the Age of Enlightenment*. Also see Olwen Hufton's voluminous history of women in western society, *The Prospect Before Her: A History of Women in Western Europe*.

Gender pay gaps: see Joanna Williams' *Women vs Feminism*.

Gender difference in sexual experience: GP Sue Turner wrote to *The Times* on 19 January 2017.

Harassment: Harriet Harman's account of being sexually propositioned appeared in her autobiography, *A Woman's Work*. Camilla Paglia's remarks on this theme are in her book, *Free Women, Free Men*. Shirley Williams' anecdote appears in Sophy Ridge's book, *The Women Who Shaped Politics*.

Historical change: Vera Brittain's account of the decline of feminism, and the rise of women's magazines focusing on housekeeping and husbands is very well described in her book, *Lady into Woman*.

Housework: Stephen Marche's theory that women fuss too much about housework appeared in *Vogue* in March 2017, derived from his book, *The Unmade Bed*. Germaine Greer's quotes come from *The Female Eunuch*.

Imperialism: I read through a copious amount of Catholic missionary magazines when I was researching a book on Irish Catholicism, and encountered articles against foot-binding in China and suttee in India. Women were often the first to convert to Christianity, perhaps for some of these reasons. As, of course, they had done in ancient Rome, according to Amaury de Riencourt's *Woman and Power in History*. Christianity's rules, he writes, though severe, 'introduced the principle of sexual equality in marriage. What was licit was licit for both sexes; what was forbidden was forbidden to both.'

Irish Women's Liberation Movement: See Anne Stopper's *Monday at Gaj's*. My own account of the train appears in *Something of Myself – and Others*, a memoir in parts, published in 2013.

Kinships: Mothers of sons: Lisa King writing in the *Daily Mail* on 6 July 2017 claims that female teachers today favour girls over boys – especially when her son missed the chance to play Oliver Twist, when Dickens' story was recast, for a school drama, as Olivia Twist. The mothers of daughters might not complain!

The *Washington Post* reported on 13 June 2016 that Harvard Business School found that fathers often advance their daughters in accomplishments.

Language issues: Sir Roger Gale's troubles were chronicled by HuffPost on 16 March 2017.

Mansplaining was coined by Rebecca Solnit, author of 'Men Explain Things To Me'.

Market value: Sienna Miller has campaigned for Hollywood pay equality for some time. On this occasion she was speaking to the *Daily Telegraph* magazine on 24 June 2017.

Marriage: Vera Brittain singles out married women as the 'chief sufferers from female subjection'.

Men excluding women: Professor Mary Beard wrote about this in the *London Review of Books* on 20 March 2014 and has been interviewed about it subsequently on several occasions.

Menstruation: See Esther Harding's *Women's Mysteries – Ancient and Modern*. *Menstrual Taboos* was a punchy little booklet produced by the Matriarchal Study Group in London in the 1970s.

Nomenclature: Sheila Michaels' obituary appeared in *The Guardian* on 7 July 2017.

Paglia and post-feminism: Apart from the quotes taken directly from her books, Camille Paglia did a sizzling live interview with Claire Fox of the Institute of Ideas on 22 October 2016.

Pregnancy experienced: See Naomi Wolf's *Misconceptions*. Dr Lisa Harris's 'Second Trimester Abortion: Breaking the Silence and Changing the Discourse', from which this except is taken, was an essay published in Reproductive

Health matters, 2008 (U.S.) and cited in *The Human Life Review*, Winter 2015.

Prohibition: See Andrew Sinclair's history.

Questions, questions: This is drawn on public debates that I have attended over the years – being a digest of the points made by pro-choice and pro-life sides (pro-choice and pro-life being self-described, duly respected). The case notes cited of reasons for late terminations were notes taken by me on the occasion when I was permitted to watch abortions at London's Samaritan Hospital (now part of St Mary's, Paddington), by Dr David Painter, the obstetrician. Professor Wendy Savage is a veteran pro-choice campaigner and her statement that sex-selective abortions should be legalised was reported in the *Independent* (and elsewhere) on 20 March 2017. The British Medical Association duly voted to remove criminal impediments to abortion which could allow termination of pregnancy up to birth on 28 July 2017. The poll about British attitudes to abortion was carried out by ComRes between 12–14 May 2017, polling 2,008 adults. The report of Italian doctors (and other European statistics) increasingly refusing to perform abortions was published in the Spring 2017 issue of the *Human Life Review*. The *Sunday Times* on 5 Mach 2017 reported on the remarkable progress in the health and survival rate of babies born at 23 weeks' gestation in Britain (the abortion limit being legally 24 weeks).

Rape and alcohol: *The Times* 22 April 2017.

Reproductive rights: Ariel Levy also writes with lucidity about this issue in *The Rules do Not Apply*, when she miscarried a much-wanted pregnancy.

Science studies: The evolutionary psychologist assesses this situation in his book, *The Blank State*.

Sexual consent law: *The Irish Times*, 20 November 2016. Further analysis: *Irish Independent*, 25 January 2017.

Soldier women: General Richard Kemp opposed women in the front line in *The Times* on 18 November 2014. Military historian Max Hastings's comments were sent to me personally.

Prudes: Laura Freeman was writing in *The Spectator* on 22 April 2017.

Transgender issues: Julie Bindel has made this point at several reprises, most recently in the *Mail on Sunday* on 2 July 2017. Ariel Levy's account of Caster Semenya is a compassionate yet honest about the difficulties in the sports field around transgender women.

Zita: St Zita's modest life is chronicled in the invaluable *Penguin Dictionary of the Saints* (Third Edition, compiled by Donald Attwater with Catherine Rachel John) and in Michael Walsh's *Dictionary of Christian Biography*.

Other material is either drawn on personal experience or available in the public realm.

Acknowledgements

Many thanks to my publishers, New Island Books, and notably to Edwin Higel, its founder, to whom Irish authors owe so much, and to Dan Bolger, the positive-thinking publisher, for their encouragement for my testament on feminism. I'm also grateful to my brilliant agent Louise Greenberg, and to Shauna Daly, who has been such an excellent editor of this book – how helpful it is to work with a clever young woman who can see these issues from her generation's viewpoint. Special thanks also to the wonderful Mariel Deegan, the designer at New Island.

I would like to pay tribute to those surviving original members of the Irish Women's Liberation Movement, who gather together for our annual veteran feminists' lunch, a tolerant and good-humoured occasion: salutations to Nell McCafferty, Eimer Philbin Bowman, Máirín de Burca, Maureen Johnston, Marie McMahon, Mary Sheerin, Rosita Sweetman and Margaret MacCurtain.

I also much appreciate conversations I've had with Dr Philbin Bowman about Irish women and the medical profession.

Thanks to Margaret Martin of Women's Aid in Dublin and Simone George of Safe Ireland for their knowledge of the sombre field of domestic violence. And to my son Ed West for producing the UN statistics which show, so surprisingly, that it's the developed societies which are sometimes the worst offenders.

Thanks to Laura Freeman for her *Spectator* essay on iPhone sexting, which I'm too old to know much about myself. Thanks also to the woman army officer, who has chosen not to be named, but who gave such a vivid and honest account of serving in the military.

Any errors, howlers or misrememberings are of course mine.

Special thanks to my cousin Brendan O'Reilly and his wife Martine who gave me much valued practical help in my personal life during the last phases of writing this book.